W9-CFS-762

Study Guide

Jan Mendoza

Golden West College
Huntington Beach, California

Understanding Psychology

SIXTH EDITION

CHARLES G. MORRIS

University of Michigan

ALBERT A. MAISTO

University of North Carolina at Charlotte

PRENTICE HALL
Upper Saddle River, New Jersey 07458

© 2003 by PEARSON EDUCATION, INC.
Upper Saddle River, New Jersey 07458

All rights reserved

10 9 8 7 6 5 4 3 2 1

ISBN 0-13-045476-1

Printed in the United States of America

TABLE OF CONTENTS

How To Use
This Study Guide

Preface

Your Time Is Valuable

Invest your study time so you get the greatest benefit!

The following techniques have been shown to increase a student's mastery of new information:

- Use as many of your senses and abilities as possible-writing, reading, hearing, speaking, drawing, etc.

- Organize information so it is meaningful to you.

- Study with other people whenever possible.

- Have FUN. We remember what we enjoy.

This study guide has been designed to provide you with ideas and resources in all of these areas. This preface explains how to effectively use the sections in each chapter.

1 The Science of Psychology

CLASS AND TEXT NOTES

This section is designed so you can take notes on these pages during lecture and also from your reading of the text. Most students find it useful to read the text and make notes before the instructor covers the material in class.

Before you begin filling out this section decide how you will tell the difference between:
- your ideas
- lecture notes
- concepts from the text
- topics emphasized on the exam

Multiple Choice Posttest

Practice exams are an important way to check your progress. The questions in your textbook after each section measure your starting point and the questions in the Posttest in the study guide measure how far you have progressed toward your goal of mastering the material.

Short Essay Questions

Many college courses are designed to help you develop your writing skills so completing short essay questions can be useful. This is especially true if your psychology course will include essay exams. You will find these questions on the Learning Objectives page.

Learning Objectives and Questions

After you have read and studied each chapter, you should be able to complete the learning objectives and short essay questions. Your exams are written based on the learning objectives so it is important to practice writing them.

Language Support

The *Language Support* section contains words students have identified from the text as needing more explanation. This section is for anyone who can benefit from extra support in English.

This page can be cut out, folded in half, and used as a bookmark in the appropriate chapter.

Most students have trouble finding enough time to study. Try carrying these flash cards with you so if you ever have to wait you can pull out a couple of cards and make good use of your time. Flash cards can also serve a very useful function during times of stress. Stress is much worse when we feel overwhelmed; in fact, we tend to shut down and do nothing. At those times divide up what you have to do and do a small portion every day. Studying 10 flash cards today is less overwhelming than thinking about the 100 pages on your next exam.

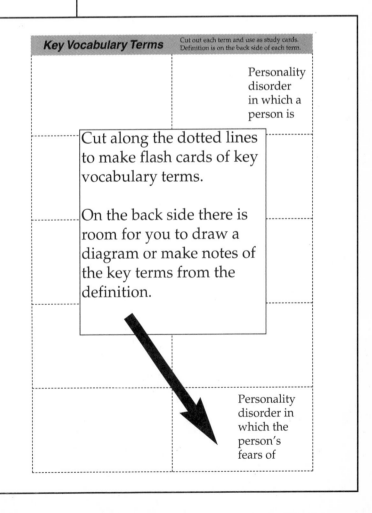

Key Vocabulary Terms   Cut out each term and use as study cards. Definition is on the back side of each term.

Personality disorder in which a person is

Cut along the dotted lines to make flash cards of key vocabulary terms.

On the back side there is room for you to draw a diagram or make notes of the key terms from the definition.

Personality disorder in which the person's fears of

STUDY TIPS

Improving Your Memory

1. Learn general information first and then specific.

2. Make material meaningful to you.

3. Create associations with what you already know.

4. Learn it actively.

5. Imagine vivid pictures.

6. Recite out loud.

7. Reduce noise and interruptions.

8. Overlearn the material.

9. Be aware of your attitude toward information.

10. Space out learning over several days.

11. Remember related information when you are having trouble recalling something.

12. Use mnemonic devices (rhymes or words created from material).

13. Combine several of these techniques at once.

Memorizing Complex Information

There are memory techniques that make learning easier and faster. One technique, known as the "loci memory system," involves picturing yourself in a familiar setting and associating it with something you need to learn. Let's assume that you needed to memorize the function and structure of a neuron. Begin by picturing yourself walking into the entry hall of your home. At the same time pretend that you are walking through a dendrite. As you walk down the hall toward the living room, imagine that you are traveling in the dendrite to the cell body. As you exit the living room and walk down the hall toward the bedrooms, think of traveling down an axon toward the terminal button that contains the neurotransmitter. In this example you are connecting new information with something very familiar. We recall information much better when we involve our imagination. An even better way to perform this exercise would be to actually walk through your home while you visualize the parts of a neuron. In this situation you would not only be using your imagination but at the same time doing something physically. It is important to realize that we have strong memories for what we do physically. Just think how long you have remembered how to ride a bike even though you may not have ridden a bike for years.

When and How to Study

1. Plan two hours study time for every hour you spend in class.
2. Study difficult or boring subjects first.
3. Avoid long study sessions.
4. Be aware of your best time of day.
5. Use waiting time by studying flash cards.
6. Use a regular study area.
7. Don't get too comfortable.
8. Use a library.
9. Take frequent breaks.
10. Avoid noise distractions.

Study in Groups

Research has shown that one of the most effective ways to learn is to study with other students. Your grades on exams will be better and you will have a lot more fun doing it!

How to Form a Group

1. Look for dedicated students who share some of your academic goals and challenges.
2. You could write a note on the blackboard asking interested students to contact you, or pass around a sign-up sheet before class.
3. Limit groups to five or six people.
4. Test the group by planning a one-time-only session. If that session works, plan another.

Some Activities for a Study Group

1. Compare notes.
2. Have discussions and debates about the material.
3. Test each other with questions brought to the group meeting by each member.
4. Practice teaching each other.
5. Brainstorm possible test questions.
6. Share suggestions for problems in the areas of finances, transportation, child care, time scheduling, or other barriers.
7. Develop a plan at the beginning of each meeting from the list above or any ideas you have.

Better Test Taking

1. Predict the test questions. Ask your instructor to describe the test format-how long it will be, and what kind of questions to expect (essay, multiple choice, problems, etc.).

2. Have a section in your notebook labeled "Test Questions" and add several questions to this section after every lecture and after reading the text. Record topics that the instructor repeats several times or goes back to in subsequent lectures. Write down questions the instructor poses to students.

3. Arrive early so you can do a relaxation exercise.

4. Ask about procedure for asking questions during test.

5. Know the rules for taking the test so you do not create the impression of cheating.

6. Scan the whole test immediately. Budget your time based on how many points each section is worth.

7. Read the directions slowly. Then reread them.

8. Answer easiest, shortest questions first. This gives you the experience of success and stimulates associations. This prepares your mind for more difficult questions.

9. Next answer multiple-choice, true-false, and fill-in-the-blank questions.

10. Use memory techniques when you're stuck.
    - If your recall on something is blocked, remember something else that's related.
    - Start from the general and go to specific

11. Look for answers in other test questions. A term, name, date, or other fact that you can't remember might appear in the test itself.

12. Don't change an answer unless you are sure because your first instinct is usually best.

Tips on Test Taking

Multiple-choice questions

1. Check the directions to see if the questions call for more than one answer.

2. Answer each question in your head before you look at the possible answers, otherwise you may be confused by the choices.

3. Mark questions you can't answer immediately and come back to them if you have time.

4. If incorrect answers are not deducted from your score, use the following guidelines to guess:
   - If two answers are similar, except for one or two words, choose one of these answers.
   - If two answers have similar sounding or looking words, choose one of these answers.
   - If the answer calls for a sentence completion, eliminate the answers that would not form grammatically correct sentences.
   - If answers cover a numerical range, choose one in the middle.
   - If all else fails, close your eyes and pick one.

True-False Questions

1. Answer these questions quickly.

2. Don't invest a lot of time unless they are worth many points.

3. If any part of the true-false statement is false, the whole statement is false.

4. Absolute qualifiers such as "always" or "never" generally indicate a false statement.

Machine-Graded Tests

1. Check the test against the answer sheet often.

2. Watch for stray marks that look like answers.

Open-Book and Notes Tests

1. Write down key points on a separate sheet.

2. Tape flags onto important pages of the book.

3. Number your notes, write a table of contents.

4. Prepare thoroughly because they are usually the most difficult tests.

Essay Questions

1. Find out precisely what the question is asking. Don't explain when asked to compare.

2. Make an outline before writing. (Mindmaps work well.)

3. Be brief, write clearly, use a pen, get to the point, and use examples.

Reading for Remembering

1. **Skim**
   Skim the entire chapter.

2. **Outline**
   Read the outline at the front of the chapter in the text.

3. **Questions**
   Write out several questions that come to your mind that you think will be answered in the chapter.

4. **Read**
   Read material with the purpose of answering your questions, critical evaluation, comprehension and practical application.

5. **Highlight**
   While reading highlight the most important information (no more than 10 percent).

6. **Answers**
   As you read, get the answers to your questions.

7. **Recite**
   When you finish reading an assignment, make a speech about it. Recite the key points.

8. **Review**
   Plan your first review within 24 hours.

9. **Review again**
   Weekly reviews are important perhaps only four or five minutes per assignment. Go over your notes. Read the highlighted parts of your text. Recite the more complicated points.

More about review

You can do short reviews anytime, anywhere, if you are prepared. Take your text to the dentist's office, and if you don't have time to read a whole assignment, review last week's assignment. Conduct five minute reviews when you are waiting for water to boil. Three-by-five cards work well for review. Write ideas and facts on cards and carry them with you. These short review periods can be effortless and fun.

Anxiety Interferes with Performance

Do you freeze up on exams, worry that you won't do well? We can turn one exam into a "do or die" catastrophic situation. Yes, we should try our best but we are not doomed for life if we fail at something. Perhaps the following examples will help you see a failure for what it is, just one more step in the process of life.

- Einstein was four years old before he could speak and seven before he could read.
- Isaac Newton did poorly in grade school.
- Beethoven's music teacher once said of him, "As a composer he is hopeless."
- When Thomas Edison was a boy, his teachers told him he was too stupid to learn anything.
- Woolworth got a job in a dry goods store when he was 21, but his employers would not let him wait on a customer because he "didn't have enough sense."
- A newspaper editor fired Walt Disney because he had "no good ideas".
- Leo Tolstoy flunked out of college.
- Louis Pasteur was rated as "mediocre" in chemistry when he attended college.
- Abraham Lincoln entered the Black Hawk War as a captain and came out as a private.
- Winston Churchill failed the sixth grade.

Failures mean very little in the big picture of our life. It is just important that we keep trying.

Effective Note-Taking During Class

1. **Review the textbook chapter before class.**
   Instructors often design a lecture based on the assumption that you have read the chapter before class. You can take notes more easily if you already have some idea of the material.

2. **Bring your favorite note-taking tools to class.**
   Make sure you have pencils, pens, highlighter, markers, paper, note cards, or whatever materials you find useful.

3. **Sit as close to the instructor as possible.**
   You will have fewer distractions while taking your notes.

4. **Arrive to class early.**
   Relax and get your brain "tuned-up" to the subject by reviewing your notes from the previous class.

5. **Picture yourself up front with the instructor.**
   The more connected you feel to the material and the instructor, the more you will understand and remember the topic.

6. **Let go of judgments and debates.**
   Focus on understanding what the instructor is saying because that is what you will find on the test. Do not get distracted by evaluating the instructor's lecture style, appearance, or strange habits. When you hear something you disagree with, make a quick note of it and then let it go.

7. **Be active in class.**
   It is the best way to stay awake in class! Volunteer for demonstrations. Join in class discussions.

8. **Relate the topic to an interest of yours.**
   We remember things we are most interested in.

9. **Watch for clues of what is important.**
   - repetition
   - summary statements
   - information written on the board
   - information the instructor takes directly from his or her notes
   - notice what interests the instructor

When Instructors Talk Too Fast

1. Read the material before class.

2. Review notes with classmates.

3. Leave large empty spaces in your notes.

4. Have a symbol that indicates to you that you have missed something.

5. Write down key points only and revise your notes right after class to add details.

6. Choose to focus on what you believe to be key information.

7. See the instructor after class and fill in what you missed.

8. Ask the instructor to slow down if you think that is appropriate.

1
The Science of Psychology

Use this section for class and text notes. Distinguish between lecture notes, textbook concepts, topics emphasized on the exam, and your own ideas.

1.   What is Psychology?   page 3

   A. The Fields of Psychology   page 4

- Developmental Psychology

- Physiological Psychology

- Experimental Psychology

- Personality Psychology

- Clinical and Counseling Psychology

- Social Psychology

- Industrial and Organization (I/O) Psychology

B. Enduring Issues   page 7

- • Person–Situation

- • Nature–Nuture

- • Stability–Change

- • Diversity–Universality

- • Mind–Body

C. Psychology As Science   page 9

- • Scientific Method

  - – Collecting Data

  - – Systematic Observation

  - – Generating Theory to Explain Data

  - – Producing Testable Hypotheses Based on the Theory

  - – Testing the Hyptheses Empirically

  - – Used to describe, understand, and predict

Critical Thinking: A Fringe Benefit of Studying Psychology

1.   Define the problem or the question you are investigating.

2.   Suggest a theory or a reasonable explanation for the problem.

3.   Collect and examine all the avilable evidence.

4.   Analyze assumptions.

5.   Avoid oversimplifying.

6.   Draw conclusions carefully.

7.   Consider every alternative interpretation.

8.   Recognize the relevance of research to events and situations.

---

2.   The Growth of Psychology   page 12

Indicate A, B, C, D or E and write the correct name of each psychologist below his picture

1. _____   2. _____   3. _____   4. _____   5. _____

A. Wilhelm Wundt: Structuralism

B. William James: Functionalism

C. Sigmund Freud: Psychodynamic Psychology

D. John B. Watson: Behaviorism

E. B.F. Skinner: Behaviorism Revisited

F. Gestalt Psychology

G. Existential and Humanistic Psychology

H. Cognitive Psychology

I. Evolutionary Psychology

J. Positive Psychology

K. Multiple Perspectives of Psychology Today

L. Where Are the Women?

---

3. Human Diversity   page 22

A. Gender

B. Race and Ethnicity

C. Culture

---

4. Research Methods in Psychology   page 28

A. Naturalistic Observation

B. Case Studies

C. Surveys

D. Correlational Research

E. Experimental Research

- Subject or participants

- Independent variable

- Dependent variable

- Experimental group

- Control group

- Experimenter bias

F. Multimethod Research

G. Importance of Sampling

- Random sample

- Representative sample

H. Human Diversity and Research

- Avoiding cultural bias

5. Ethics and Psychology   page 37

   A. Ethics in Research on Humans

   - Informed of nature of research

   - Informed consent documented

   - Risks and limits on confidentiality explained

   - Alternative academic credit so truly free choice for students

   - Deception restricted

   B. Ethics in Research on Nonhuman Animals

---

6. Careers in Psychology   page 40

   A. Academic and Applied Psychology

   B. Clinical Settings

After you have read and studied this chapter, you should be able to complete the following statements. Your exam is written based on these learning objectives.

LEARNING OBJECTIVES

1. Describe the major subdivisions of psychology including developmental, physiological, experimental, personality, clinical and counseling, social, and industrial/organizational psychology.

2. Define psychology and explain the role played by the scientific method in psychological research, including the four goals of psychologists.

3. Summarize the five enduring issues of psychology.

4. Describe the early schools of psychology (Structuralism, Functionalism, Psychoanalysis, Behaviorism) and their founders.

5. Distinguish between the five basic research methods used by psychologists to gather information about behavior and give an example of a situation in which each method would be used appropriately.

6. Discuss cognitive psychology, how it differs from behaviorism and its impact on the field of modern psychology.

7. Explain the importance of human diversity for researchers and how a lack of understanding of diversity, lack of diversity and cultural bias can affect research results.

8. Discuss the ethical concerns in psychology and how they affect both humans and animals in research and treatment.

9. List the differences in training and activities of psychiatrists, counseling and clinical psychologists, psychoanalysts and social workers.

SHORT ESSAY QUESTIONS

1. Describe the importance of sampling related to issues of gender, race and culture in research.

2. Explain Milgram's study, why it was so controversial, how it affected the APA's ethical guidelines and the issue of deception and punishment in psychological research.

3. Discuss the differences between structuralism and functionalism; behaviorism and cognitive psychology and how Freud's psychoanalytic differed from these schools.

4. Discuss the design of an experiment studying the effects of alcohol on aggressive behavior. Label the hypothesis, independent variable, dependent variable, control and experimental group and the measures taken to avoid experimental bias.

5. Define the terms: sample, population, random sample and representative sample. Explain how researchers can overcome obstacles to obtaining a good sample.

6. Explain the goals and interests of evolutionary psychologists and give two examples of the types of findings they have uncovered.

7. Describe the role played by women in the history of psychology, some obstacles that have prevented women from achieving equal status with males and the current status of women in psychology.

8. Define and discuss the emerging field of positive psychology and its unique perspective on mental wellness as opposed to mental illness.

Language Support

Students identified the following words from the text as needing more explanation. This page can be cut-out, folded in half, and used as a bookmark for this chapter.

A

Adherents of	those who believe in, devoted followers of
Advocate	speak, plead or argue in favor of
Affiliate with	accept as a member, associate or branch of
Against all odds	surprisingly winning over major difficulties
Anonymity	unknown or unacknowledged name, authorship or agency
Ascribe	attribute to a specific cause, source or origin
Assimilate	include, absorb, accept, make similar to

B

Blank slate	unmarked surface, 'tabula rasa'
Blunder	make a mistake, to flounder
Breadth	wide range or scope

C

Colleague	people who work together, associates, companions
Commingle	mix together
Competent	well qualified, adequate or properly trained for the purpose
Conjecture	inference based on incomplete evidence, guess
Constraints	restrictions, limitations, restraints
Contradict	to deny, discrepancy, to say something that doesn't agree
Controversial	dispute between sides, holding opposing views
Criteria	standard or basis for making a judgment

D

Decorum	behavior within social conventions
Derive	obtain from a source, originate, deduce or infer
Devote	dedicate, give oneself totally to
Differentiate	perceive a distinction or difference between
Discrete	individually distinct, keep separate
Dissimilar	different or distinct, not alike
Distinct	of marked difference, clear, well defined
Distinguish	observe the difference between, keep apart, discern
Dominate	influence strongly

E

Elicit	to bring or draw out, call for, evoke
Embedded	insert, enclose, locate or fix in surrounding area
Emergence	to come forth into view, come into existence or notice
Empower	to invest with power or authority
Encounter	meet face to face, confront
Encompass	include or contain
Enduring issues	topics that sustain interest, continue or last over time
Establish	set up, settle, make stable, prove, institute or verify
Evolve	develop gradually, unfold naturally
Expel	drive or force out
Explicit	fully and clearly expressed, defined or formulated
Extent	degree, scope or range to which something extends

F

Fascinate	intense interest or attraction
Faulty generalization	deciding without gathering all the facts or prematurely
Flair for	talent or aptitude, instinctive discernment
Formulate	to express, state or prepare in systematic terms
Fundamental	essential, basic, involving all aspects, of central importance

G

Ghetto	inner city neighborhood occupied by minority groups, slum
Grasp	understanding, comprehension

H

Holistic	interdependence and importance of all the parts of a whole
Heresy	controversial opinion in opposition to tradition

I

Impartial	unbiased, unprejudiced, neutral
Improvise	make up, invent or recite without preparation
Inaccessible	unapproachable, not having entry point or opening
Infamous	having a bad reputation, notorious
Inference	conclude from evidence or premises
Influential	exerting influence or power, important
Inhumane	cruel, without compassion or feeling
Initiative	ability to begin or follow through with a plan or task
Intercede	mediate, act as a go between
Intervene	come between, alter or hinder an event or action
Investigate	examine thoroughly, inquire into
Irrelevant	unrelated to the matter at hand
Ivy league	prestigious, traditional colleges mostly on East Coast

L

Liaison	communication between groups, rendezvous or meeting
Loopholes	opening in premise or law allowing another interpretation

M

Magna cum laude	graduating with high honors
Mean streets	dangerous neighborhood
Miracle cure	medical discovery considered very helpful, wonder drug
Monopolize	dominate by excluding others
Morale	state of mind of person or group, spirit of the group
Mutual	shared, have in common

O

Obsolete	no longer in use or needed, outmoded
Opponent	against another or others, opposite viewpoint or stance
Orthodox	adhering to traditional, accepted ways
Over request	asking for too much
Override	to prevail over, set aside, consider more important than
Overwhelmingly	overpowering, irresistible, to decisively, strongly

P

Penchant	preference, strong inclination, definite liking
Phenomena	unusual fact or occurrence
Pioneer	innovator especially in research and development
Precursor	one that comes before, indicates or announces something
Predisposed	inclined to something in advance, susceptible or likely
Prohibitions	forbidding by law, taboo, not allowed
Prestigious	prominent, distinguished, respected
Prevalent	widely occurring, common

Prominence	widely known, eminent
Proximity	closeness, nearness
Puzzled	confused or baffled by, bewildered by
R	
Realm	area, field or location
Reassign	transfer from one location or task to another
Repertoire	range of skills, aptitudes or accomplishments
Resurface	come out at another time
S	
Scrutiny	very close look, examine carefully
Shed light on	help to understand more clearly
Sentient	conscious, perceptive and alert beings
Skeptical	doubt, question or disagree
Stringent	vigorous or severe standards
Superstition	irrational belief or practice in magical or chance happening
Supplant	supercede, take place instead of
T	
Transform	change markedly in form, nature, appearance or condition
U	
Underlying	basic, fundamental, implicit, present but not obvious
V	
Voodoo	using fetishes, spells, curses, magical power or deception
Vulnerable	susceptible to attack, easily affected, not protected
W	
Wooed	seeking to gain or achieve, seeking romantic affection
Y	
Yield	give way to pressure, force or persuasion, give in return
Z	
Zapped	exposure to electric current or radiation

Multiple Choice Posttest

After studying the text and completing the Study Guide activities, answer these questions to determine if you need to review any areas before the course exam.

1. Psychology is the science of _____.
   a. Behavior and mental processes
   b. Objective introspection
   c. Inductive reasoning
   d. Emotions

2. Psychologists use the scientific method to do each of the following except ____ what they study.
   a. Describe
   b. Circumvent
   c. Predict
   d. Control

3. The scientific method has been applied to psychological issues for about the last ____ years.
   a. 100
   b. 200
   c. 300
   d. 400

4. A specific, testable prediction about a phenomenon, usually derived from a theory, is a _____.
   a. Thesis
   b. Hypothesis
   c. Principle
   d. Prognosis

5. The basic atoms or units of experience and their combinations were the foundation of ____.
   a. Functionalism
   b. Structuralism
   c. Behaviorism
   d. Psychoanalysis

6. Consciousness as a continuous flow is an important concept to ____.
   a. Structuralism
   b. Functionalism
   c. Objective introspection
   d. Behaviorism

7. Freud's theories differed radically from the views of American psychologists of the time because of _____.
   a. Its extensive use of laboratory research to support its claims
   b. The emphasis it placed on Eastern philosophies and culture
   c. The emphasis it placed on unconscious processes
   d. Its emphasis on environmental learning as the source for most personality characteristics

8. The idea that psychology should be based only on observable, measurable behaviors is central to _____.
   a. Behaviorism
   b. Cognitive theory
   c. Structuralism
   d. Psychodynamic theory

9. Gestalt theory emphasizes _____.
   a. Flow of consciousness
   b. The atoms of thought
   c. Environmental stimuli
   d. Our tendency to see patterns

10. The scientific study of the ways in which people perceive, interpret, store, and retrieve information is central to _____ psychology.
    a. Humanistic
    b. Behavioral
    c. Existential
    d. Cognitive

11. Research that observes behavior in its actual setting without controlling anything is called _____.
    a. Correlational method
    b. Naturalistic observation
    c. Survey research
    d. Case study method

12. The _____ is a detailed description and analysis of a single individual or a few individuals and may include a variety of information gathering methods.
   a. Correlational method
   b. Naturalistic observation
   c. Survey research
   d. Case study method

13. The degree of relationship between two or more variables is _____.
   a. Correlation
   b. Naturalistic observation
   c. Reliability
   d. Synchronicity

14. The only research method that can demonstrate a cause and effect relationship between variables is the _____ method.
   a. Correlational
   b. Naturalistic observation
   c. Survey research
   d. Experimental

15. A researcher manipulates the _____ variable to see how it affects a second variable.
   a. Placebo
   b. Independent
   c. Dependent
   d. Correlational

16. A sample carefully chosen so that the characteristics of the subjects correspond closely to the characteristics of the general population is known as a _____ sample.
   a. Random
   b. Controlled
   c. Biased
   d. Representative

17. Subjects in Milgram's studies were told they were taking part in studies on ___ but were really being tested on ____.
   a. learning, biofeedback
   b. pain thresholds, biofeedback
   c. learning, obedience
   d. obedience, learning

18. Milgram's studies on obedience raised significant controversy regarding _____.
   a. The quality of laboratory equipment used in psychological research
   b. Laboratory research on human sexuality
   c. The use of placebo techniques to treat severe psychological disorders
   d. Ethics and the use of deception in research

19. Which of the following mental health professionals is the only one who can prescribe medicine?
   a. A psychologist
   b. A social worker
   c. A counselor
   d. A psychiatrist

20. The process involved in critical thinking is very similar to the process involved in ____.
   a. Eastern philosophy
   b. Objective introspection
   c. The scientific method
   d. Common sense

Answers and Explanations to Multiple Choice Posttest

1. a. Psychology is the science of behavior and mental processes. p. 3

2. b. The second goal of psychology is to explain behavior. p. 10

3. a. It was in the late 1800's that the scientific method was applied to questions about human behavior and mental processes. p. 13

4. b. A hypothesis is a testable prediction about the phenomenon in question. p. 10

5. b. Structuralism focuses on basic units or atoms of experiences and their combinations. p. 13

6. b. Consciousness as a continuous flow is important to functionalism. pp. 13–14

7. c. Freud believed that people are motivated by unconscious instincts and urges. p. 15

8. a. Behaviorists believed that psychology was the study of observable, measurable behavior-and nothing more. p. 14–15

9. d. Gestalt theory emphasizes our tendency to see patterns. p. 16–17

10. d. Cognitive psychology is the study of mental processes in the broadest sense. p. 17–18

11. b. Naturalistic observation involves watching a research subject in the natural setting. p. 28

12. d. A case study is a detailed description of one person or a few individuals and may include real life observation, interviews, psychological test scores, and interviews with others. p. 29–30

13. a. Correlational research is based on a naturally occurring relationship between two variables. pp. 30–32

14. d. Only the experimental method can prove cause and effect. pp. 32–33

15. b. A researcher manipulates the independent variable. p. 33

16. d. A representative sample is carefully chosen to correspond closely to the characteristics of the larger population. p. 35

17. c. Milgram's subjects were told the research was about learning but it was really about obedience. p. 37

18. d. Milgram's study sparked such a public uproar that the APA was forced to reassess its ethical guidelines. p. 38

19. d. Psychiatrists are medical doctors and the only mental health professional s licensed to prescribe medication. p. 40

20. c. Critical thinking requires thinking like a scientist similar to the steps of the scientific method. p. 11

Key Vocabulary Terms

Cut out each term and use as study cards.
Definition is on the back side of each term.

Psychology	Structuralism
Scientific method	Functionalist theory
Theory	Psychodynamic theories
Hypotheses	Behaviorism
Representative sample	Gestalt psychology

School of psychology that stresses the basic units of experience and the combinations in which they occur.

The scientific study of behavior and mental processes.

Theory of mental life and behavior that is concerned with how an organism uses its perceptual abilities to function in its environment.

An approach to knowledge that relies on collecting data, generating a theory to explain the data, producing testable hypotheses based on the theory and testing those hypotheses empirically.

Personality theories contending that behavior results from psychological factors that interact within the individual, often outside conscious awareness.

Systematic explanation of a phenomenon; it organizes known facts, allows us to predict new facts, and permits us to exercise a degree of control over the phenomenon.

School of psychology that studies only observable and measurable behavior.

Specific, testable predictions derived from a theory.

School of psychology that studies how people perceive and experience objects as whole patterns.

Sample carefully chosen so that the characteristics of the subjects correspond closely to the characteristics of the larger population.

Existential psychology	Culture
Humanistic psychology	Race
Cognitive psychology	Ethnicity
Evolutionary psychology	Positive Psychology
Gender	Naturalistic observation

The tangible goods produced in a society, and the values, attitudes, behaviors, and beliefs that are passed from one generation to another.

School of psychology that focuses on the meaninglessness and alienation of modern life and how these factors lead to apathy and psychological problems.

A subpopulation of a species, defined according to an identifiable characteristic (i.e., geographic location, skin color, hair texture, genes, facial features).

School of psychology that emphasizes nonverbal experience and altered states of consciousness as a means of realizing one's full human potential.

A common cultural heritage, including religion, language, ancestry, that is shared by a group of individuals.

School of psychology devoted to the study of mental processes in the broadest sense.

The view that psychology should devote more attention to the "good life" and the origins and nurgturance of mental wellness rather than mental illness.

An approach and subfield of psychology concerned with the evolutionary origins of behaviors and mental process, their adaptive value, and the purposes they continue to serve.

Research method involving the systematic study of animal or human behavior in natural settings rather than in the laboratory.

The psychological and social meanings attached to being biologically male or female.

Observer bias	Participants
Case study	Independent variable
Survey research	Dependent variable
Correlational research	Experimental group
Experimental method	Control group

Individuals whose reactions or responses are observed in an experiment.

Expectations or biases of the observer that might distort or influence his or her interpretation of what was actually observed.

In an experiment, the variable that is manipulated to test its effects on the other, dependent variables.

Intensive description and analysis of single individual or just a few individuals.

In an experiment, the variable that is measured to see how it is changed by manipulations in the independent variable.

Research technique in which questionnaires or interviews are administered to a select group of people.

In a controlled experiment, the group subjected to a change in the independent variable.

Research technique based on the naturally occurring relationship between two or more variables.

In a controlled experiment, the group not subjected to a change in the independent variable; used for comparison with the experimental group.

Research technique in which an investigator deliberately manipulates selected events or circumstances and then measures the effects of those manipulations on subsequent behavior.

Experimenter
bias

Random
sample

	Expectations by the experimenter that might influence the results of an experiment or its interpretation.
	Sample in which each potential subject has an equal chance of being selected.

2

The Biological Basis of Behavior

C L A S S   A N D   T E X T   N O T E S

Use this section for class and text notes. Distinguish between lecture notes, textbook concepts, topics emphasized on the exams and your own comments.

1. Neurons: The Messengers   page 48

   A. Dendrites

   B. Axon

   C. Nerve or tract

   D. Myelin sheath

   E. Support cells—Glial cells

D. Synaptic Vesicles

E. Neurotransmitters

- Acetylcholine (ACH)

- Dopamine

- Serotonin

- Endorphins

F. Receptor Sites

---

4. Neural Plasticity and Neurogenesis   page 54

A. Neural Plasticity

B. Neurogenesis

---

5. The Central Nervous System   page 57

A. Spinal Cord

B. The Brain

- Brain Stem

- Medulla

- Pons

- Cerebellum

- Midbrain

- Thalamus

- Hypothalamus

- Reticular formation

- Limbic system

- Cerebral Hemispheres

  - Association areas

  - Occipital Lobe

  - Temporal Lobe

  - Parietal Lobe

  - Frontal Lobe

C. Hemisphereic Specialization   page 62

- Corpus Callosum

- Left Hemisphere Dominance

- Right Hemisphere Dominance

- Split-brain patients

D. Tools for Studying the Brain   page 65

- Microelectrode Techniques

- Macroelectrode Techniques

- Structural Imaging

    – Computerized Axial Tomography (CAT or CT scan)

    – Magnetic Resonance Imaging (MRI)

- Functional Imaging

  - EEG imaging

  - Magnetoencephalography (MEG)

  - Positron emission tomography scanning (PET)

  - Functional magnetic resonance imaging (fMRI)

F. The Pancreas

F. The Pituitary Gland

G. The Gonads

H. The Adrenal Glands

---

10. Genes, Evolution, and Behavior   page 73

- Behavior Genetics

- Evolutionary Psychology

A. Genetics

- Genes

- Chromosomes

- Deoxyribonucleic acid (DNA)

- Human Genome

- Dominant gene

- Recessive gene

- Polygenic Inheritance

B. Behavior Genetics

- Human Genome

- Animal behavior genetics

  - Heritability

  - Strain studies

  - Selection studies

- Human Behavior genetics

  - Family studies

  - Twin studies

  - Identical twins

  - Fraternal twins

  - Adoption studies

- Molecular Genetics

- Evolutionary Psychology

  - Natural selection

- Social Implications

Learning Objectives and Questions

After you have read and studied this chapter, you should be able to complete the following statements. Your exam is written based on these learning objectives.

LEARNING OBJECTIVES

1. Describe the structure of the neuron. Trace the path of a neural impulse and explain how it transmits messages from one neuron to another.

2. Describe the process by which a neuron moves from a resting state to firing and then back to a resting state.

3. Describe the effects of the neurotransmitters acetylcholine, dopamine, serotonin, norepinephrine, and endorphins.

4. Describe the location and function of the medulla, cerebellum, thalamus, hypothalamus, and cerebral cortex.

5. Describe the functions of the frontal lobe, temporal lobe, occipital lobe and parietal lobes of the brain.

6. Compare and contrast the functions of the left and right hemispheres of the cerebral cortex. What role does the corpus callosum play in this functioning?

7. Compare and contrast the functions of the sympathetic and parasympathetic nervous system.

8. Describe the basic functions of the endocrine system, including the specific functions of the thyroid gland, pancreas, pituitary gland, gonads, and adrenal glands.

9. Define genes, chromosomes, and DNA and describe their role in the genetic transmission of traits.

10. Define and describe the uses for and limitations of family studies, twin studies, and adoption studies. What has been learned about the role of heredity in shaping human personality?

11. Discuss the field of evolutionary psychology and identify the types of human behaviors that interest evolutionary psychologists. Briefly discuss the criticisms of this field and how evolutionary psychologists respond to these criticisms.

12. Discuss The Human Genome project and its contribution to understanding genetics and mapping the chromosomes. Give at least two examples of traits or diseases that have been identified and marked on the human chromosomes.

SHORT ESSAY QUESTIONS

1. Discuss how cocaine, curare, caffeine, opiates, and LSD block or disrupt neural communication. Which receptor sites do these drugs specifically affect?

2. What are the reasons for, and the results of, split brain operations? What is the difference between split-brain surgery and hemispherectomies?

3. Briefly describe the functions of the reticular formation, the limbic system, and the spinal cord. What kind of problems can result from damage or destruction of these areas?

4. Briefly discuss the purposes of and procedures for studying the brain within each of the following general areas: microelectrode techniques; macro electrode techniques; structural imaging, functional imaging.

5. Compare and contrast strain studies and selection studies. What are they used for and what has been learned from them. Discuss any limitations of these techniques.

6. Identify and briefly explain the four major principles of Darwin's theory of natural selection. What scientific fields have been impacted by his ideas and how large has that impact been?

7. Discuss some social implications of behavior genetics.

8. Identify several approaches to studying heritability of a trait.

9. Explain the concepts of dominant and recessive genes and discuss how a child's eye color may be influenced if the father has blue eyes and the mother has brown eyes.

10. Briefly summarize the research regarding stem cells and the possibility of growing new neurons in the human brain. Define neuronal plasticity and neurogenesis. Which specific disorders or diseases may be helped by this method?

11. What are some of the ethical concerns regarding stem cell research and development?

Language Support

Students identified the following words from the text as needing more explanation. This page can be cut-out, folded in half, and used as a bookmark for this chapter.

A

Aftereffects	delayed or prolonged response to a stimulus
Astonished	fill with or cause wonder, amazement or surprise
Artificial	made to imitate something in nature, not genuine
Assumption	accept as true without proof
Attention deficit	unable to concentrate due to impulsiveness and inattention
Attraction	arouse the interest, admiration or attention of

B

| Bizarre | strikingly unconventional, odd or weird |
| Boost | increase, lift, raise up |

C

Cadaver	dead body, often used for dissection (autopsy)
Cite	quote as authority, use as support, proof or to illustrate
Clone	replica or copy of a DNA sequence, closely resemble
Concentrate	focus, direct thoughts or attention to something
Continuous	uninterrupted in time, sequence, substance or extent
Coordinate	to harmonize in a common action or effort

D

Delayed onset	to postpone or begin at a later time
Deleterious	harmful, dangerous, injurious
Deliberately	action done with full awareness of the effect, intentional
Destiny	predetermine course of events, inevitable fate
Dexterity	skill in the use of one's body, hands or mind
Dilemma	a situation that requires a choice between options
Disrupt	break apart, throw into confusion, stop or interrupt
Docile	easily managed or taught
Double helix	2 coiled strands of DNA forming a spiral shape

E

Ebullient	enthusiastic, lively, bubbly
Enable	supply with means or knowledge, make possible
Environment	surroundings, circumstances or conditions around one
Equilibrium	balance between opposing forces, influences or actions
Equivalent	equal, similar or identical in form or effect
Exceed	go beyond the limits, surpass
Exhibit	to show or display
Exterminate	destroy completely, wipe out

F

| Facet | an aspect, part or one side of |
| Facilitate | to assist or make easier |

H

Hastily	rapid, speedy action made to quickly to be accurate
Harvest	result or consequence of an activity
Heighten	intensify, increase or strengthen in quality or degree

I

Impaired	diminished or weakened functioning
Implied	express or indicate indirectly, suggest
Impoverished	deprive of strength or nourishment, poverty
Inaugurate	begin or introduce formally
Inbred	mating of closely related individuals
Indirectly	not straight to the point, diverging from plan or course
Induce	persuade or move to action, influence
Ingenious	imaginative, resourceful, clever
Insulate	protective covering to prevent loss of heat, sound, etc.
Integrate	join together, unify, unite without restriction
Interplay	reciprocal action and reaction, interaction
Interpret	explain or clarify meaning based upon one's understanding
Intricate	having complex elements, requiring effort to understand
Intriguing	arousing interest or curiosity
Irreverent	disrespectful act or remark

K

Keen	intellectually sharp or sensitive, enthusiastic

L

Landmark	historically significant event or location

M

Merge	blend together or be absorbed, often gradually
Migraine	severe, recurring headache often affecting one side of head
Misguided	led in the wrong direction or astray
Minute (my-nute)	exceptionally small, beneath notice, insignificant, tiny
Mysterious	something that is unexplainable or not fully understood

N

Notion	idea, whim or impulse, belief or opinion

O

Obstinate	difficult to manage, control or subdue, stubborn
Opposite effect	sharply contrasting results or outcomes
Origin	ancestry, point at which something comes into existence

P

Paradigm	example that serves as a pattern or model
Patent	invention protected by a grant
Perpetuate	prolong the existence or duration of
Pinpoint	to locate, target or identify with precision
Pioneer	innovator in research and development
Plausible	believable, apparently true or likely, credible
Predominate	controlling power or influence, greater importance
Primitive vertebrates	animals with simple body structure
Profane	irreverent, contempt for what is sacred, vulgar language
Prognosis	prediction of possible or probable outcome
Promising	likely to develop favorably
Provocative	inciting anger or resentment, stirring up action or feelings

R

Replicate	duplicate, copy, repeat or reproduce itself (DNA)
Reveal	to show, bring to view or light

S

Sequentially	following one after another in time or continuous series
Shallow	lacking depth of intellect, emotion or knowledge
Spark	to set in motion or spur

Strenuous	requiring great effort, energy or exertion
Specialized	to choose or adapt to a specific function or field of study
Spontaneously	arising without apparent external cause or thought
Subdue	to quiet or bring under control, make less intense
Subtle	difficult to detect, not obvious, requiring fine distinction
Susceptibility	likelihood of being influenced, allowing or permitting
Sustain	maintain, provide with necessities to survive, support
T	
Tamper	interfere with harmfully or meddle
Temperament	one's nature or character
Tendency	inclination to think, act or behave a certain way
Three-dimensional	extending in depth, width and height in space and time
U	
Urgency	requiring immediate action
V	
Voluntary	using free will or volition, intentionally, deliberately
W	
Wander	lose clarity of thought, go astray, to move aimlessly

Multiple Choice Posttest

After studying the text and completing the Study Guide activities, answer these questions to determine if you need to review any areas before the course exam.

1. The term "plasticity" as it regards the brain, refers to _____.
   a. brittleness or rigidity
   b. levels of complexity
   c. softness or crevices
   d. ability to adapt to new conditions

2. The field of psychobiology explores the ways in which ____.
   a. biological processes affect our behavior
   b. our mental state affects our physical health
   c. behavioral patterns affect biological development
   d. evolution has shaped our instincts, drives, urges and needs

3. The smallest unit of the nervous system and the cell that underlies the activity of the entire nervous system is the _____.
   a. glial cell
   b. epidermal cell
   c. neuron
   d. T-cell

4. Neurons that receive information from sensory organs and relay that information to the spinal cord and the brain are called _____.
   a. association neurons
   b. efferent neurons
   c. afferent neurons
   d eons

5. When a neuron is polarized, _____.
   a. potassium ions pass freely through the cell membrane
   b. the electrical charge inside is positive relative to the outside
   c. it cannot fire
   d. the electrical charge inside is negative relative to the outside

6. The entire area composed of the axon terminal of one neuron, the synaptic cleft, and the dendrite or cell body of the next neuron is called the
   a. synaptic vesicle
   b. synaptic knob
   c. synaptic space
   d. synapse

7. The "all or none" law refers to _____.
   a. a group of neurons firing together
   b. a neuron fires at full strength or not at all
   c. all the dendrites must be receiving messages telling the neuron to fire or it will not fire at all
   d. all the neurons in a single nerve fire simultaneously

8. People with Parkinson's disease and schizophenia probably have a deficiency of the neurotransmitter _____.
   a. norepinephrine
   b. serotonin
   c. dopamine
   d. acetylcholine

9. Morphine and other opiates are able to bind to the receptor sites for _____.
   a. acetylcholine
   b. hypothalamus
   c. dopamine
   d. endorphins

10. Eating, drinking, sexual behavior, sleeping and temperature control are regulated by the _____.
    a. thalamus
    b. hypothalamus
    c. cerebral cortex
    d. corpus callosum

11. The part of the brain most people think of when they talk about the brain is the _____.
    a. cerebral cortex
    b. pons
    c. medulla
    d. cerebellum

12. What structure connects the two hemispheres of the brain and coordinates their activities?
    a. reticular formation
    b. amygadala
    c. hippocampus
    d. corpus callosum

13. The part of the brain that helps regulate hearing, balance and equilibrium, certain emotions and motivation and recognizing faces is the _____.
    a. occipital lobe
    b. temporal lobe
    c. parietal lobe
    d. frontal lobe

14. A part of the brain that sends the signal "Alert" to higher centers of the brain in response to incoming messages is
    _____.
    a. limbic system
    b. reticular formation
    c. amygdala
    d. hippocampus

15. The thyroid gland controls _____.
    a. glucose absorption
    b. emotions
    c. metabolism
    d. sexuality

16. The _____ hemisphere of the cerebral cortex is usually dominant in spatial tasks while the _____ hemisphere usually dominant in language tasks.
    a. frontal, lateral
    b. left, right
    c. right, left
    d. lateral, frontal

17. The limbic system is responsible for _____.
    a. controlling learning and emotional behavior
    b. providing a bridge for numerous brain areas
    c. analyzing problematic situations
    d. fighting pathogens

18. The system that coordinates and integrates behavior by secreting chemicals into the bloodstream is called the _____.
    a. somatic system
    b. autonomic system
    c. limbic system
    d. endocrine system

19. The endocrine glands located just above the kidneys that release hormones important for dealing with stress are the _____.
    a. gonads
    b. adrenal glands
    c. parathyroid glands
    d. pituitary glands

20. The complex molecule that forms the code for all genetic information is the _____.
    a. DNA
    b. messenger RNA
    c. RNA
    d. monoamine oxidase

21. _____ is a test on a fetus to determine if there are any genetic abnormalities.
    a. amniocentesis
    b. positron emission tomography
    c. magnetic resonance
    d. CT-scans

22. Which of the following would provide the best map of physical structures in the brains of living human beings?
    a. magnetic resonance imaging (MRI)
    b. magnetoencephalography (MEG)
    c. positron emission tomography (PET) scan
    d. electroencephalography (EEG) imaging

23. The term that refers to the full complement of an organism's genetic material is _____.
    a. gender
    b. genome
    c. heritability
    d. polygenetic inheritance

24. Studies of heritability in humans that assume that if genes influence a certain trait, close relatives should be more similar with that trait than distant relatives are called _____.
    a. family studies
    b. twin studies
    c. strain studies
    d. selection studies

25. Research on human brain tissue has found that human adult brains ____ have stem cells and neurogenesis ____ occur in human adult brains.
    a. do not, does not
    b. do, does not
    c. do not, does
    d. do, does

Answers and Explanations to Multiple Choice Posttest

1. d. Plasticity in the human brain is the ability to adapt to new environmental conditions. p. 47

2. a. Psychobiology is the branch of psychology that deals with the biological basis of behavior and mental processes. p. 47

3. c. A neuron is the smallest unit of the nervous system and underlies the activity of the entire nervous system. p. 48

4. c. Afferent (sensory) neurons carry messages from sense organs to the spinal cord or brain. p. 48

5. d. When the electrical charge inside the neuron is negative relative to the outside, it is called polarized or polarization. p. 49

6. d. A synapse is composed of the axon terminal of one neuron, the synaptic space and the dendrite or cell body of the next neuron. p. 51

7. b. The all-or-none law operates on the principle that the action potential in a neuron either fires at full strength or not at all. p. 51

8. c. The neurotransmitter dopamine is involved in a wide variety of behaviors and emotions and is implicated in schizophrenia and Parkinson's disease. p. 52

9. d. Opiates such as morphine and heroin bind to the receptor sites for endorphins and shed information on addictive behavior. p. 53

10. b. Portions of the hypothalamus govern hunger, thirst, sexual drive, body temperature, rage, terror and pleasure. p. 59

11. a. Most people think of or refer to the cerebral cortex when talking about 'the brain'. p. 59

12. d. The corpus callosum is a thick, ribbonlike band of nerve fibers that is the primary connection between the left and right hemispheres. p. 62

13. b. The temporal lobe of the brain regulates hearing, balance, equilibrium, some emotions and motivation and facial recognition. p. 61

14. b. The reticular formation's main job is to send "alert!" signals to the higher brain in response to incoming messages. p. 59

15. c. The thyroid gland regulates the body's rate of metabolism and how alert and energetic people are. p. 71

16. c. The right hemisphere tends to dominate in spatial and holistic tasks the left hemisphere tends to dominate in language and sequential activities. p. 63

17. a. The limbic system plays a role in learning and emotional behavior and forming new memories. p. 62

18. d. The endocrine system secretes hormones into the bloodstream that coordinate and integrate behavior. p. 70–71

19. b. The adrenal glands (adrenal cortex and adrenal medulla) affect the body's reaction to stress by releasing hormones into the bloodstream. p. 73

20. a. Deoxyribonucleic acid (DNA) is a complex, double helix shaped molecule that is the main ingredient of chromosomes and genes and forms the code for all genetic information. p. 74

21. a. Amniocentesis is a prenatal screening procedure that harvests cells taken from the amniotic fluid to determine defects. p. 80

22. a. (MRI) Magnetic resonance imaging observes computerized colored brain images to detect abnormal brain activity and map structures in the brain. p. 67

23. b. A genome is the complete set of an organism's genetic material. p. 74

24. a. Family studies assume that close relatives should have more heritability than distant relatives on certain traits. p. 82

25. d. Major breakthrough research in 1998 has proven that adult brains do have stem cells and that neurogenesis does occur in human adult brains. pp. 56–57

Key Vocabulary Terms

Cut out each term and use as study cards.
Definition is on the back side of each term.

Neurons	Glial cells/ glia
Dendrites	Ions
Axon	Resting potential
Nerve or tract	Polarization
Myelin sheath	Neural impulse or action potential

Cells that insulate and support neurons by holding them together, providing nourishment, removing waste products, preventing harmful substances from passing into the brain, and forming the myelin sheath.

Individual cells that are the smallest unit of the nervous system.

Electrically charged particles found both inside and outside of the neuron.

Short fibers that branch out from the cell body and pick up incoming messages.

Electrical charge across a neuron membrane resulting from more positive ions concentrated on the outside and more negative ions on the inside.

Single long fiber extending from the cell body; it carries outgoing messages.

The condition of a neuron when the inside is negatively charged relative to the outside; when the neuron is at rest.

Groups of axons bundled together.

The firing of a nerve cell.

White fatty covering found on some axons.

Graded potential	Terminal button or synaptic knob
Threshold of excitation	Synaptic space or synaptic cleft
Absolute refractory period	Synapse
Relative refractory period	Synaptic vesicles
All-or-none law	Neurotransmitters

Structure at the end of an axon terminal branch.

A shift in the electrical charge in a tiny area of a neuron.

Tiny gap between the axon terminal of one neuron and the dendrites or cell body of the next neuron.

The level an impulse must exceed to cause a neuron to fire.

Area composed of the axon terminal of one neuron, the synaptic space, and the dendrite or cell body of the next neuron.

A period after firing when a neuron will not fire again no matter how strong the incoming messages may be.

Tiny sacs in a terminal button or synaptic knob that release chemicals into the synapse.

A period after firing when a neuron is returning to its normal polarized state and will fire again only if the incoming message is much stronger than usual.

Chemicals released by the synaptic vesicles that travel across the synaptic space and affect adjacent neurons.

Principle that the action potential in a neuron does not vary in strength; either the neuron fires at full strength or it does not fire at all.

Receptor sites	Pons
Central nervous system	Cerebellum
Peripheral nervous system	Brain stem
Spinal cord	Midbrain
Medulla	Thalamus

Part of the hindbrain that connects the cerebral cortex at the top of the brain to the cerebellum.

Locations on a receptor neuron into which a specific neurotransmitter fits like a key into a lock.

Structure in the hindbrain that control certain reflexes and coordinates the body's movements.

Division of the nervous system that consists or the brain and spinal cord.

The top of the spinal column; it widens out to form the hindbrain and midbrain.

Division of the nervous system that connects the central nervous system to the rest of the body.

Region between the hindbrain and the forebrain; it is important for hearing and sight, and it is one of several places in the brain where pain is registered.

Complex cable of neurons that runs down the spine, connecting the brain to most of the rest of the body.

Forebrain region that relays and translates incoming messages from the sense receptors, except those for smell.

Part of the hindbrain that controls such functions as breathing, heart rate, and blood pressure.

Hypothalamus	Temporal lobe
Cerebral hemisphere	Parietal lobe
Cerebral cortex	Frontal lobe
Association areas	Corpus callosum
Occipital lobe	Reticular formation

Part of the cerebral hemisphere that helps regulate hearing, balance and equilibrium, and certain emotions and motivations.	Forebrain region that governs motivation and emotional responses.
Part of the cerebral cortex that receives sensory information from throughout the body.	The largest part of the brain, developed more in humans than in any other animal.
Part of the cerebral cortex that is responsible for voluntary movement; it is also important for attention, goal-directed behavior, and appropriate emotional experiences.	The outer surface of the two cerebral hemispheres that regulate most complex behavior.
A thick band of nerve fibers connecting the left and right cerebral cortex.	Areas of the cerebral cortex where incoming messages form the separate senses are combined into meaningful impressions and outgoing messages from the motor areas are integrated.
Network of neurons in the hindbrain, midbrain, and part of the forebrain whose primary function is to alert and arouse the higher parts of the brain.	Part of the cerebral hemisphere that receives and interprets visual information.

Limbic system	Sympathetic division
Somatic nervous system	Parasympathetic division
Afferent neurons	Hormones
Efferent neurons	Endocrine glands
Autonomic nervous system	Thyroid gland

Branch of the autonomic nervous system, it prepares the body for quick action in an emergency.

Ring of structures that plays a role in learning and emotional behavior.

Branch of the autonomic nervous system; it calms and relaxes the body.

The part of the peripheral nervous system that carries messages from the senses to the central nervous system and between the central nervous system and the skeletal muscles.

Chemical substances released by the endocrine glands; they help regulate bodily activities.

Sensory neurons that carry messages from sense organs to the spinal cord or brain.

Glands of the endocrine system that release hormones into the bloodstream.

Motor neurons that carry messages from the spinal cord or brain to the muscles and glands.

Endocrine gland located below the voice box; it produces the hormone thyroxin.

The part of the peripheral nervous system that carries messages between the central nervous system and the internal organs.

Parathyroids	Adrenal glands
Pineal gland	Genes
Pancreas	Nature versus nurture
Pituitary gland	Genetics
Gonads	Heredity

Two endocrine glands located just above the kidneys.	Four tiny glands embedded in the thyroid; they secrete parathormone.
Elements that control the transmission of traits; they are found on the chromosomes.	A gland located roughly in the center of the brain that appears to regulate activity levels over the course of a day.
A debate surrounding the relative importance of heredity (nature) and environment (nurture) in determining behavior.	Organ lying between the stomach and small intestine; it secretes insulin and glucagon, to regulate blood sugar levels.
Study of how traits are transmitted from one generation to the next.	Gland located on the underside of the brain; it produces the largest number of the body's hormones.
The transmission of traits from one generation to the next.	The reproductive glands–testes in males and ovaries in females.

Chromosomes	Polygenic inheritance
Deoxyribonucleic acid (DNA)	Behavior genetics
Traits	Evolutionary psychology
Dominant gene	Heritability
Recessive gene	Family studies

Process by which several genes interact to produce a certain trait; responsible for our most important traits.

Pairs of threadlike bodies within the cell nucleus that contain the genes.

Study of the relationship between genetics and behavior.

Complex molecule in a double-helix configuration that is the main ingredient of chromosomes and genes and forms the code for all genetic information.

A subfield of psychology concerned with the origins of behaviors and mental processes, their adaptive value, and the purposes they continue to serve.

Characteristics on which organisms differ.

The extent to which variations in a trait can be attributed to genetic factors.

Member of a gene pair that controls the appearance of a certain trait.

Studies of heritability in humans based on the assumption that if genes influence a certain trait, close relatives should be more similar on that trait than distant relatives.

Member of a gene pair that can control the appearance of a certain trait only if it is paired with another recessive gene.

Twin studies	Psychobiology
Identical twins	Interneurons (association) neurons
Fraternal twins	Primary motor cortex
Adoption studies	Human genome
Natural selection	Hindbrain

The area of psychology that focuses on the biological foundations of behavior and mental processes.	Studies of identical and fraternal twins to determine the relative influence of heredity and environment on human behavior.
Neurons that carry messages from one neuron to another.	Twins developed from a single fertilized ovum and therefore identical in genetic makeup at the time of conception.
The section of the frontal lobe responsible for voluntary movement.	Twins developed from two separate fertilized ova and therefore different in genetic makeup.
The full complement of genes within a human cell.	Research carried out on children adopted at birth by parents not related to them, to determine the relative influence of heredity and environment on human behavior.
Area containing the medulla, pons, and cerebellum.	The mechanism proposed by Darwin in his theory of evolution, which states that organisms best adapted to their environment tend to survive, transmitting their genetic characteristics to offspring.

Label Drawings

Label the parts of a neuron.

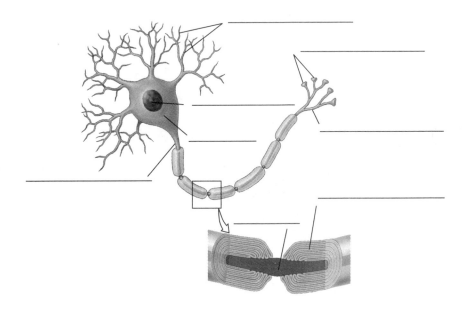

Label the parts of the neuron at the synapse.

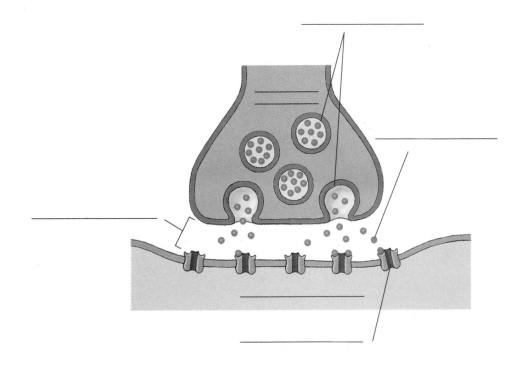

Name each lobe of the brain and identify the parts of the brain.

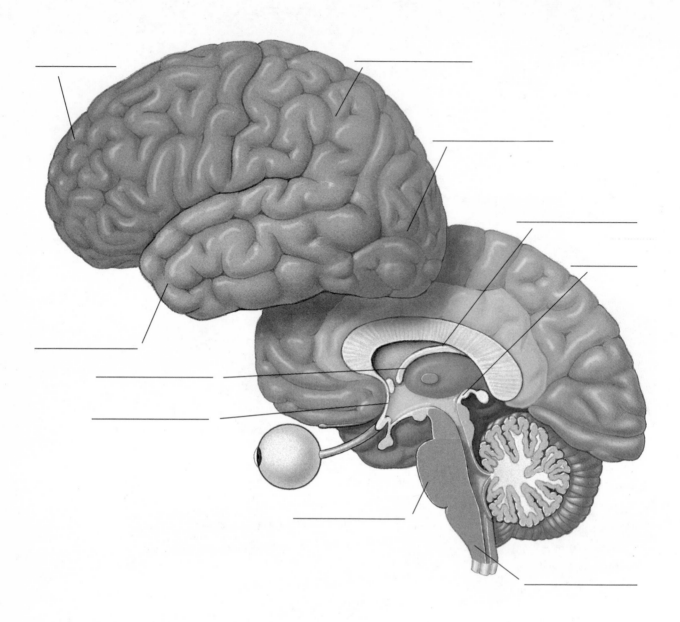

3

Sensation and Perception

CLASS AND TEXT NOTES

Use this section for class and text notes. Distinguish between lecture notes, textbook concepts, topics emphasized on the exams and your own comments.

1. The Nature of Sensation   page 88

    A. The Character of Sensation

    - Receptor Cell

    - Doctrine of Specific Nerve Energies

    B. Sensory Thresholds

    - Absolute threshold

    - Adaptation

    - Difference threshold or just noticeable difference (jnd)

    - Weber's law

C. Subliminal Perception

- Advertisements

  - Self-Help tapes

UNDERSTANDING THE WORLD AROUND US page 91

Does Extrasensory Perception Exist?

- ESP

- Telepathy

- Parapsychology

---

2. Vision page 92

A. The Visual System

- Cornea

- Pupil

- Iris

- Lens

- Retina

- Fovea

- The Receptor Cells

  - Wavelengths

  - Rods

  - Cones

  - Bipolar cells

  - Visual acuity

- Adaptation

  - Dark adaptation

  - Light adaptation

  - Afterimage

- From Eye to Brain

  - Ganglion cells

  - Optic nerve

  - Blind spot

  - Optic chaism

B. Color vision

- Properties of color

  - Hue

  - Saturation

  - Brightness

- Theories of color vision

  - Additive Color Mixing

  - Subtractive Color Mixing

  - Trichromatic (3 Color) theory

  - Colorblindness

    1. Trichromats

    2. Dicromats

    3. Monochromats

C. Color Vision in Other Species

3.   Hearing   page 101

A. Sound

- Sound waves

- Frequency

- Hertz (Hz)

- Pitch

- Amplitude

- Decibels

- Overtones

- Timbre

B.   The Ear

- Outer ear

- Middle Ear

  – Hammer

  – Anvil

  – Stirrup

- Inner Ear

- Oval window

- Cochlea

- Basilar membrane

- Organ of Corti

- Auditory Nerve

- Neural Connections

C. Theories of Hearing

- Place Theory

- Frequency Theory

- Volley principle

- Hearing disorders

    - Deafness

    - Tinnitus

    - Remedies

---

4. The Other Senses   page 106

A. Smell

- Detecting common odors

- Olfactory bulb

- Pheromones

B. Taste

- Taste buds

C. Kinesthetic and Vestibular Senses

- Kinesthetic Senses

- Stretch receptors

- Golgi tendon organs

- Vestibular senses

- Vestibular sacs

UNDERSTANDING OURSELVES   page 110

The Importance of Touch

– Closure

– Continuity

B. Perceptual Constancies

- Size constancy

- Shape constancy

- Color constancy

- Brightness constancy

C. Perceptions of Distance and Depth

Monocular cues

- Interposition

- Linear perspective

- Aerial perspective

- Elevation

- Texture gradient

- Shadowing

- Motion parallex

Binocular cues

- Stereoscopic vision

- Retinal disparity

- Convergence

D. Location of Sounds

- Monaural cues

- Binaural cues

E. Perception of Movement

- Real movement

- Apparent movement

- Autokinetic illusion

- Stroboscopic motion

- Psi phenomenon

F. Visual Illusions

- Real world illusions

- Physical illusion

- Perceptual illusion

- Induced movement

G. Observer Characteristics

- Motivation

- Values

- Expectations

- Cognitive Style

- Experience and Culture

- Personality

Learning Objectives and Questions

After you have read and studied this chapter, you should be able to complete the following statements. Your exam is written based on these learning objectives.

LEARNING OBJECTIVES

1. Compare and contrast sensation and perception and describe the events that produce each of them.

2. Describe the difference between the absolute threshold and difference threshold and how consistent these thresholds are across people, place and time.

3. Describe the process of adaptation. Discuss light and dark adaptation and the phenomenon of afterimages.

4. Explain how messages entering the eye are processed in the brain.

5. Describe the two main theories of color vision.

6. Identify the characteristics of sound.

7. Describe the structure of the ear and explain the functions of the various parts.

8. State the two theories of pitch discrimination.

9. Summarize the theories that explain how the sense of smell is activated by chemical substances and describe the role smell plays in our daily lives.

10. Explain the processes involved in the sense of taste and name the four primary qualities of taste.

11. Explain how the sensations of pressure, warmth and cold originate and how people respond to them.

12. Discuss three theories of pain: gate control theory, biopsychosocial theory and placebo effect. Describe the role played by endorphins and people's subjective experience of pain.

13. Define perceptual constancy and identify four kinds.

14. Describe four observer characteristics that can affect perception.

15. Identify the contributions of both monocular and binocular cues of depth.

SHORT ESSAY QUESTIONS

1. Define pitch, amplitude, decibels, overtones, and timbre.

2. Differentiate between hue, brightness and saturation. Explain the difference between additive and subtractive color mixing.

3. Distinguish between rods and cones and list their characteristics and functions with respect to light, color and how they connect to other cells.

4. Describe hearing disorders and explain the causes of deafness and tinnitus.

5. Describe autokinetic illusion, stroboscopic movement, the phi phenomenon and the illusion of induced movement.

6. Explain subliminal perception and discuss research findings on the effectiveness of subliminal messages on people's behavior.

7. Explain extrasensory perception, telepathy and clairvoyance. Define parapsychology and discuss research findings in this field.

8. Describe how we use monoaural and binaural cues to locate the source of sounds.

9. Discuss the principles of perceptual organization identified by the Gestaltists.

10. Compare and contrast real and apparent movement and provide three examples of apparent movement.

Language Support

Students identified the following words from the text as needing more explanation. This page can be cut-out, folded in half, and used as a bookmark for this chapter.

A

Adage	traditional saying about a common experience or observation
Adept	very skillful, proficient, expert
Ad campaign	media plan to promote, make known or sell
Ambiguous	having several possible meanings or interpretations
Ancestry	one's lineage or the origin of an idea, object or phenomenon
Apparent	obvious, easily understood
Assess	estimate the value of, determine, judge the value or character of
Assume	take for granted without proof, suppose
Attune	bring into harmony or relationship with, adjust

B

Bland	not highly flavored, mild, lacking in interest
Blip	brief interruption, short erratic movements, spot of light on screen
Blotches	large irregular spot or stain
Blurred	make indistinct, smudge, smear
Bombard	to attack vigorously
Bypass	to avoid or circumvent by going around, neglect or ignore opinion

C

Characteristic	typical of, distinctive quality or feature
Coherent	logically connected, consistent, harmonious
Collision	clash, conflict, forceful impact
Consequent	following as the result or logical conclusion
Contend	hold or maintain a position; struggle or oppose
Contour	outline of a figure, edge or defining line
Contradictory	inability of opposing view or evidence to be true or false
Conversely	opposite or contrary in direction, action or sequence
Convey	communicate, move
Correspond	agree or conform with, match
Cue	guiding suggestion, stimulate to action, sensory signal
Customary	long continued practice according to custom or habit

D

Decipher	make meaning of something difficult to understand
Defect	shortcoming, imperfection, weakness
Displace	remove, replace or move out of usual place or position
Discrepancy	difference, inconsistency, disagreement
Dramatically	vivid, highly compelling or effective

E

Ebb	decline, decay, fade, flow backward or away
Enhance	magnify the intensity, increase in quality, degree or value, improve
En route	on or along the way
Evidence	support for a belief, that which proves or disproves something
Exclusively	excluding or limiting; singularly, reserved for something alone
Excruciating	causing intense suffering, torment or torturous action
Exert	put forth into vigorous action or effort

F

Fateful	of great significance, controlled by fate or destiny
Feat	noteworthy or extraordinary act or achievement
Flexible	easily modified, adaptable
Fooled	tricked, deceived or imposed on
Foreknowledge	knowing something before it happens, foresee
Fraction	small portion or segment of a whole

H

Hazy	vague, misty, indefinite
Hidden	concealed from sight, obstructed, covered up, kept secret
Hypersensitive	excessively affected by external influences or emotions

I

Implant	insert, plant or establish firmly
In sync	in agreement with, at the same time and rate, together
Interpretation	assigning meaning or understanding of something
Interrelated	reciprocal, in mutual association or connection between or among
Irresistible	tempting, unable to oppose
Irreversible	incapable of being changed

L

Limbo	intermediate, transitional or midway state or place

M

Manipulate	influence or change something to suit one's purpose or advantage
Mimic	to imitate or copy

O

Optimally	most favorable condition for obtaining desired results
Overall	covering or including everything

P

Particular	specific, exceptional, separately, distinct
Pedestrian	person traveling on foot; lacking in distinction or imagination
Perplexing	puzzling or bewildering, uncertainty, confused
Pool	to join together in common interest, combine
Precisely	specifically, exactly, fixed
Predatory	preying upon others, greedy, selfish
Pretend	to make believe, false appearance, deceive
Prompt	quick to act or respond, on time, assist by suggestion
Protracted	drawn out, lengthen, prolong
Pygmy	of small size or stature, African tribe of tiny people

Q

Quiver	to shake, slight but rapid motion, tremble

R

Radical	drastic, extreme, having strong convictions
Rarely	exceptional, unusual, infrequent
Realistic	based on what is practical or actual, representing what 'is'
Relevant	having practical value, applicable, pertinent to the matter at hand
Remarkable	worthy of note, unusual
Remedy	counteract, something that cures, corrects or relieves
Resonate	echo or ring with sound, amplify or sustain sound

S

Sophisticated	worldly wise, intricate, complex
Sparse	thinly scattered or distributed, scanty, meager
Speculate	think curiously about, reflect, to wonder
Stationary	not moving, standing still, fixed position
Sufficient	adequate, enough

T

Tactile	having to do with the sense of touch
Transpose	change or reverse position, order or sequence, interchange
Transmute	change from one substance, condition or form into another

U

Uncanny	extraordinary, mysterious, having an unexplainable basis
Unique	unusual, not typical, no equal, sole example

V

Vice versa	reverse order from the preceding statement, conversely
Vintage	high quality of past time, classic

Multiple Choice Posttest

After studying the text and completing the Study Guide activities, answer these questions to determine if you need to review any areas before the course exam.

1. Sensation is to _____ as perception is to _____.
   a. Stimulation; interpretation
   b. Interpretation; stimulation
   c. Sensory ability; sensory acuity
   d. Sensory acuity; sensory ability

2. The _____ is reached when a person can detect a stimulus 50 % of the time.
   a. Difference threshold
   b. Just noticeable difference threshold
   c. Absolute threshold
   d. Separation threshold

3. Which of the following is NOT true of subliminal perception?
   a. The effects attributed to subliminal perception may be the results of conscious expectations.
   b. Subliminal messages may be able to change attitudes.
   c. People can perceive stimuli they cannot consciously describe.
   d. It works equally as well in all people.

4. _____ are receptor cells in the retina responsible for night vision and perceiving brightness and _____ are receptor cells in the retina responsible for color vision.
   a. Rods; cones
   b. Rods; reels
   c. Cones; rods
   d. Cornea; iris

5. The ability of the eye to distinguish fine details is called _____.
   a. Visual dilation
   b. Visual acuity
   c. Visual sensitivity
   d. Adaptation

6. On the chart below, label the energies in the electromagnetic spectrum in order: FM radio waves, AC circuits, X-rays; radar, TV radio waves, infrared rays, gamma rays, AM radio waves, ultra violet rays.

7. Motion sickness arises in the _____.
   a. Kinesthetic organs
   b. Cutaneous organs
   c. Cerebral cortex
   d. Vestibular organs

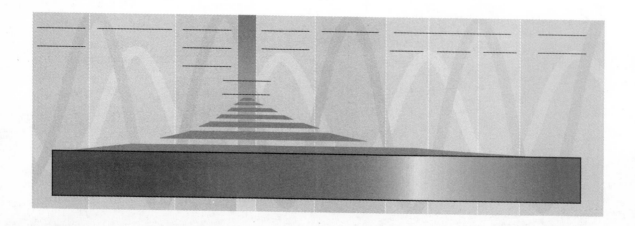

8. The process of mixing various pigments together to create different colors is called _____.
   a. Blending
   b. Trichromatic color mixing
   c. Subtractive color mixing
   d. Additive color mixing

9. The psychological experience created by the brain in response to changes in air pressure that are perceived in the auditory system is known as _____.
   a. vibration
   b. harmonics
   c. sound
   d. amplitude

10. On the chart below, label the amount of decibels of the following common sounds. Patter of rain; revolver firing at close range; subway train; normal conversation; whisper; average office interior; sonic boom; power lawnmower, food blender; air raid siren; live rock music; heavy truck; leaves rustling; window air conditioner, heavy truck, air raid siren, jet plane/personal stereo; pain threshold, potential ear damage; heavy traffic/vacuum/dishwasher.

11. Hertz is a unit of measurement of _____.
    a. the timbre of a sound
    b. how high or low a sound is
    c. the frequency of a sound
    d. the amplitude of a sound

12. A chemical that communicates information to other organisms through the sense of smell is called _____.
    a. A saccule
    b. A pheromone
    c. Odorant protein binding
    d. A scent

13. Flavor is _____.
    a. A combination of texture and taste
    b. A combination of taste and smell
    c. A combination of texture and smell
    d. Taste

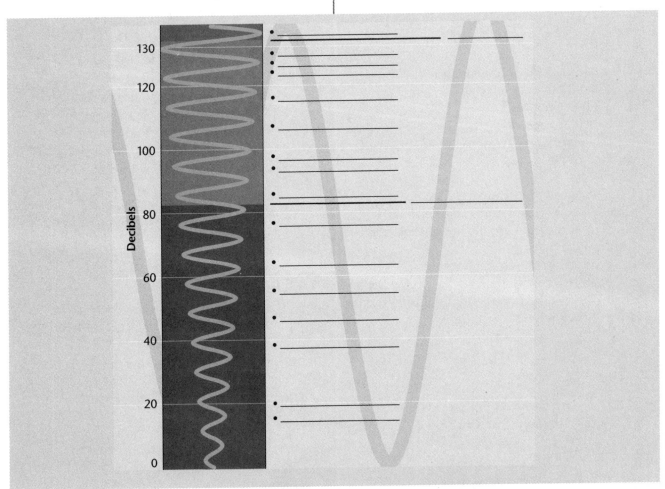

14. The _____ has the most numerous receptors.
    a. Eye
    b. Ear
    c. Nose
    d. Skin

15. Optical illusions result from distortion in _____.
    a. transduction
    b. sensation
    c. perception
    d. adaptation

16. You know a house is the same size whether you are standing right next to it or a mile away from it because of _____.
    a. phi phenomenon
    b. the figure-ground distinction
    c. retinal disparity
    d. perceptual constancy

17. Our general method for dealing with the environment is known as _____.
    a. intelligence
    b. perceptual style
    c. personality
    d. cognitive style

18. Visual distance and depth cues that require the use of both eyes are called _____.
    a. Monocular cues
    b. Diocular cues
    c. Binocular cues
    d. Dichromatic cues

19. Placebo pills and acupuncture have been effective in reducing pain. The common element in these methods may be their ability to stimulate the ____.
    a. production of adrenal hormones
    b. opening of neurological gates in the spine
    c. arousal of the peripheral nervous system
    d. production of endorphins

20. The phenomenon whereby items that continue a pattern or direction tend to be grouped together as part of a pattern is _____.
    a. proximity
    b. similarity
    c. closure
    d. continuity

21. The phenomenon in which we perceive movement in objects that are actually standing still is known as _____.
    a. apparent movement
    b. real movement
    c. biological movement
    d. induced movement

22. On the chart below, match the Gestalt principles of perceptual organization with the appropriate pattern.
    a. continuity
    b. closure
    c. proximity
    d. similarity

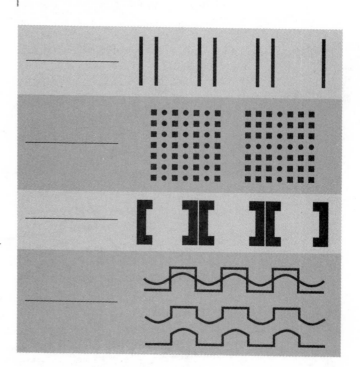

Answers and Explanations to Multiple Choice Posttest

1. a. Sensation is the stimulation of a receptor cell (p. 88) and perception is our interpretation of that stimulation (p. 112).

2. c. Absolute threshold is a sensation detected 50% of the time. p. 88

3. d. Subliminal perception has not been shown to affect everyone in the same way. p. 90

4. a. Rods are receptors for night vision and brightness, and cones are receptors for color vision. p. 94

5. b. Visual acuity refers to our ability to see fine details. p. 94

6. Fig. 3–4, p. 93. From left to right: gamma rays; x rays; ultraviolet rays (visible light); infrared rays; radar; radio waves: FM – TV – AM; AC circuits.

7. d. Motion sickness originates in the vestibular organs. p. 108

8. c. Mixing of pigments is called subtractive color mixing. p. 99

9. c. Sound is our brain's interpretation of the changes in air pressure in our eardrums. p. 101

10. Fig. 3–16, p. 102 From top to bottom: *revolver; 130 decibels: Pain Threshold; sonic boom;* air raid siren; jackhammer; @*120 decibels: jet plane/personal stereo; live rock music; 100 decibels: subway train; heavy truck;* power lawn mower/food blender; *80 decibels: Potential Ear Damage;* heavy traffic/vacuum/dishwasher; normal conversation; *60 decibels: window air conditioner;* patter of rain; *40 decibels: average office interior; 20 decibels: leaves rustling; whisper.*

11. c. Hertz refers to the frequency of the sound wave. p. 101

12. b. Pheromones are chemicals hat communicate information to other organisms through smell. p. 107

13. b. Flavor is a combination of taste and smell. p. 107

14. a. The skin is the largest sense organ and contains the most receptors. p. 109

15. c. Optical illusions are the result of distortions in perception. p. 112

16. d. Perceptual constancy enables us to see distant objects as the same size as when viewed close by. p. 115

17. d. Our cognitive style determines how we deal with our environment. p. 123

18. c. Binocular cues require both eyes. p. 117

19. d. Placebos and acupuncture both work through the release of endorphins. p. 111

20. d. Continuity is perceived as a pattern or direction of items grouped together. p. 115

21. a. Apparent motion is when we perceive movement in objects that are actually standing still. p. 119

22. Fig. 3–27, p. 115. c. proximity; d. similarity; b. closure; a. continuity

Key Vocabulary Terms

Cut out each term and use as study cards.
Definition is on the back side of each term.

Sensation	Weber's Law
Perception	Cornea
Absolute threshold	Pupil
Adaptation	Iris
Difference threshold or just noticeable difference (jnd)	Lens

The principle that the just noticeable difference (jnd) for any given sense is a constant fraction or proportion of the stimulation being judged.

Basic experience of stimulating the body's senses.

The transparent protective coating over the front part of the eye.

Process of creating meaningful patterns from raw sensory information.

Small opening in the iris through which light enters the eye.

The least amount of energy that can be detected as a stimulation 50 percent of the time.

Colored part of the eye that regulates the size of the pupil.

Adjustment of the senses to the level of stimulation they are receiving.

Transparent part of the eye behind the pupil that focuses light onto the retina.

The smallest change in stimulation that can be detected 50 percent of the time.

Retina	Bipolar Cells
Fovea	Dark adaptation
Wavelengths	Light adaptation
Rods	Afterimage
Cones	Ganglion cells

Neurons that have only one axon and one dendrite; in the eye, these neurons connect the receptors on the retina to the ganglion cells.

Lining of the eye containing receptor cells that are sensitive to light.

Increased sensitivity of rods and cones in darkness.

Area of the retina that is the center of the visual field.

Decreased sensitivity of rods and cones in bright light.

The different energies represented in the electromagnetic spectrum.

Sense experience that occurs after a visual stimulus has been removed.

Receptor cells in the retina responsible for night vision and perception of brightness.

Neurons that connect the bipolar cells in the eyes to the brain.

Receptor cells in the retina responsible for color vision.

Optic nerve	Brightness
Blind spot	Additive color mixing
Optic chiasm	Subtractive color mixing
Hue	Trichromatic theory
Saturation	Colorblindness

The nearness of a color to white as opposed to black.	The bundle of axons of ganglion cells that carries neural messages from each eye to the brain.
The process of mixing lights of different wavelengths to create new hues.	Place on the retina where the axons of all the ganglion cells leave the eye and where there are no receptors.
The process of mixing pigments, each of which absorbs some wavelengths of light and reflects others.	Point near the base of the brain where some fibers in the optic nerve from each eye cross to the other side of the brain.
Theory of color vision that all color perception derives from three different color receptors in the retina (usually red, green, and blue receptors).	The aspect of color that corresponds to names such as red, green, and blue.
Partial or total inability to perceive hues.	The vividness or richness of a hue.

Trichromats	Hertz (Hz)
Monochromats	Pitch
Dichromats	Amplitude
Opponent-process theory	Decibel
Frequency	Overtones

Cycles per second; unit of measurement for the frequency of sound waves.	People who have normal color vision.
Auditory experience corresponding primarily to frequency of sound vibrations, resulting in a higher or lower tone.	Organisms that are totally colorblind.
The magnitude of a wave; in sound, the primary determinant of loudness.	People and animals who are blind to either red-green or yellow-blue.
Unit of measurement for the loudness of sounds.	Theory of color vision that three sets of color receptors (yellow-blue, red-green, black-white) respond to determine the color you experience.
Tones that result from sound waves that are multiple of the basic tone: primary determinant of timbre.	The number of cycles per second in a wave; in sound, the primary determinant of pitch.

Timbre	Place theory
Oval window	Frequency theory
Cochlea	Volley principle
Basilar membrane	Olfactory bulb
Auditory nerve	Pheromone

Theory that pitch is determined by the location of greatest vibration of the basilar membrane.

The quality or texture of sound; caused by overtones.

Theory that pitch is determined by the frequency with which hair cells in the cochlea fire.

Membrane across the opening between the middle ear and inner ear that conducts vibrations to the cochlea.

Refinement of frequency theory; receptors in ear fire in sequence, one group, then another, etc., complete pattern of firing corresponds to the frequence of sound.

Part of the inner ear containing fluid that vibrates which in turn causes the basilar membrane to vibrate.

The smell center in the brain.

Vibrating membrane in the cochlea of the inner ear; it contains sense receptors for sound.

Chemical that communicates information to other organisms through smell.

The bundle of axons that carries signals from each ear to the brain.

Taste buds	Gate control theory
Kinesthetic senses	Perceptual constancy
Stretch receptors	Size constancy
Golgi tendon organs	Shape constancy
Vestibular senses	Brightness constancy

Theory that a "neurological gate" in the spinal cord controls the transmission of pain messages to the brain.

Strucures on the tongue that contain the receptor cells for taste.

Tendency to perceive objects as stable and unchanging despite changes in sensory stimulation.

Senses of muscle movement, posture, and strain on muscles and joints.

Perception of an object as the same size regardless of the distance from which it is viewed.

Receptors that sense muscle stretch and contraction.

Tendency to see an object as the same shape no matter what angle it is viewed from.

Receptors that sense movement of the tendons, which connect muscle to bone.

Perception of brightness as the same, even though the amount of light reaching the retina changes.

Senses of equilibrium and body position in space.

Color constancy	Elevation
Monocular cues	Texture gradient
Binocular cues	Shadowing
Linear perspective	Motion parallax
Aerial perspective	Stereoscopic vision

Monocular cue to distance and depth based on the fact that the higher on the horizonal plane an object is, the farther away it appears.	Inclination to perceive familiar objects as retaining their color despite changes in sensory information.
Monocular cue to distance and depth based on the fact that objects seen at greater distances appear to be smoother and less textured.	Visual cues requiring the use of one eye.
Monocular cue to distance and depth based on the fact that shadows often appear on the parts of objects that are more distant.	Visual cues requiring the use of both eyes.
Monocular distance cue: objects closer than point of visual focus seem to move opposite viewer's moving head, and objects beyond the focus point seem to move same direction as the viewer's head.	Monocular cue to distance and depth based on the fact that two parallel lines seem to come together at the horizon.
Combination of two retinal images to give a three-dimensional perceptual experience.	Monocular cue to distance and depth based on the fact that more distant objects are likely to appear hazy and blurred.

Retinal disparity	Stroboscopic motion
Convergence	Sound
Monaural cue	Sound Waves
Binaural cue	Organ of Corti
Autokinetic illusion	Biopsychosocial Theory

Apparent movement that results from flashing a series of still pictures in rapid succession, as in a motion picture.

Binocular distance cue based on the difference between the images cast on the two retinas when both eyes are focused on the same object.

A (psychological?) experience created by the brain in response to changes in air pressure that are received by the auditory system.

A visual depth cue that comes from muscles controlling eye movement as the eyes turn inward to view a nearby stimulus.

Changes in pressure caused when molecules of air or fluid collide with one another and then move apart again.

Cue to sound location that requires just one ear.

Structure on the surface of the basilar membrane that contains the receptor cells for hearing.

Cue to sound location that involves both ears working together.

Theory that the interaction of biological, psychological, and cultural factors influence the intensity and duration of pain.

The perception that a stationary object is actually moving.

Placebo
effect

Interposition

Phi
phenomenon

Pain relief that occurs when
a person believes a pill or
procedure will reduce pain.
The actual cause of relief
seems to come from
endorphins.

Monocular distance cue in
which one object, by
partly blocking a second
object, is perceived as
being closer.

Apparent movement
caused by flashing lights
in sequence, as on theater
marquees.

States of Consciousness

CLASS AND TEXT NOTES

Use this section for class and text notes. Distinguish between lecture notes, textbook concepts, topics emphasized on the exams and your own comments.

1.   Conscious Experience   page 130

    A. Daydreaming and Fantasy

2.   Sleep   page 132

    •   Circadian Cycles: The Biological Clock

    •   The Rhythms of Sleep

       – Alpha waves

       – Delta waves

       – Rapid Eye Movement (REM)

       – Paradoxical Sleep

       – Non-REM sleep

UNDERSTANDING The World Around Us   page 147

Binge Drinking on College Campuses

Learning Objectives and Questions

After you have read and studied this chapter, you should be able to complete the following statements. Your exam is written based on these learning objectives.

LEARNING OBJECTIVES

1. Explain the difference between waking consciousness and altered states of consciousness, providing examples of each.

2. Define daydreaming and explain the basic theories. Discuss different types of daydream themes and which kinds of daydreams may be found in healthy individuals.

3. Explain circadian rhythms and the human biological clock. How is our functioning affected by these rhythms and how disruptions in these rhythms can negatively affect people.

4. Identify the various stages of sleep and describe the physiological changes accompanying each stage. Outline the chronological sequencing and timing of sleep stages throughout the night.

5. Identify at least three sleep disorders and discuss their symptoms.

6. Summarize the research on dreams, how dreams vary among people and four proposed functions of dreaming.

7. Know the difference between substance abuse and substance dependence, tolerance, and withdrawal.

8. Discuss the difference is drugs and drug use in the past and current drugs and drug use.

9. List the seven signs of substance dependence.

10. Discuss why some people seem to be more susceptible to becoming alcoholics. Consider gender and ethnic group differences.

11. Describe the physical and psychological effects of barbiturates, opiates, caffeine, nicotine, stimulants, cocaine, LSD and marijuana and problems associated with their use.

12. Define meditation and discuss the positive and negative effects of meditation and its potential use.

13. Discuss the history and uses of hypnosis. Describe how people differ in their hypnotic susceptibility and the possible medical and therapeutic benefits of hypnosis.

SHORT ESSAY QUESTIONS

1. Discuss the research findings in regard to sleep deprivation: its prevalence, symptoms and the effects of long-term deprivation.

2. List five of the eleven signs of alcoholism.

3. Summarize the trend of 'binge drinking' on college campuses and discuss factors that may contribute to binge drinking as well as its effects.

4. Describe the effect of addictive drugs on neurotransmitters and the brain.

5. Discuss how researchers design and carry out experiments and studies of alcohol and drug use and abuse.

6. Outline the path of alcohol in the brain; list the parts of the brain affected by alcohol chronologically and why some people perceive alcohol as a stimulant.

7. Define insomnia, which it affects, what its cause is, and what steps a person can take to overcome this sleep disorder.

Language Support

Students identified the following words from the text as needing more explanation. This page can be cut-out, folded in half, and used as a bookmark for this chapter.

A

Abstinence	refrain from certain food, drugs, alcohol or behavior
Accessible	easy to approach, reach, enter, attain, understand
Accredited	officially accepted, certified, reputable
Aggravate	make worse or more severe, intensify, irritate or annoy
Appraisal	estimation or judging the nature of value, a considered opinion
At bay	keeping away difficulty or an enemy

B

Banned	to forbid, prohibit or bar, denounce, make illegal
Biopsy	removing living tissue for a diagnostic evaluation
Black market	illegal buying and selling of goods, which violates legal price controls
Bombard	attack vigorously

C

Censored	suppress or delete objectionable material; adversely criticize
Clandestine	conceal or take place in secrecy
Consumption	eat, drink, devour, use
Convivial	friendly, jovial, festive, fond of eating, drinking and partying
Counterculture	lifestyle of those who reject society's dominant values and behavior
Crave	long for, desire, require

D

Deterrent	discourage or restrain from, prevent
Disillusioned	free from illusion or conviction, disenchanted
Distort	twist out of shape, alter original appearance, misrepresent
Duration	length of time something occurs or exists

E

Epidemic	widespread, rapidly spreading, prevalent; affecting many at once
Episodically	occurring sporadically, loosely connected incident in a course of events
Escalate	increase the intensity or magnitude of
Euphoria	strong feeling of happiness, confidence or well-being

F

Fend off	resist, ward off, keep away, defend
Fleeting	vanishing quickly, passing swiftly
Folk remedy	traditional cultural medical or health practices
Fraternity	male social organization, usually on college campuses
Frenzied	wildly excited or enthusiastic; violently agitated
Frown upon	to show displeasure or disapproval, scowl

G

Glamorize	glorify or romanticize
Groggy	dazed, weakened, unsteady

H

Harbinger	announce or come before, forerunner, to herald
Hippie movement	1960's youths who rejected established society, advocated free love, expanded consciousness, unconventional dress and behavior

I

Illicit	illegal, unlawful, not permitted for moral or legal reasons
Illogical	contrary to or disregarding the laws of logic
Imbibe	consume by drinking, absorbing or soaking up
Inebriated	intoxicated, drunk, under the influence of alcohol
Interspersed	scattered or placed at intervals among other things; diversified
Ironically	coincidentally, unexpectedly

K

Kaleidoscopic	continually shifting pattern of colored glass reflected in a mirrored tube

M

Mirroring	reflecting back, faithful representation
Mishap	unfortunate accident
Monotonous	lacking in variety, tedious, boring, repetitive

N

Notion	generalized, vague concept, idea or belief; a foolish whim

O

Off the record	confidential; not to be published or quoted

P

Pacifier	nipple shaped device that babies suck on while teething
Paved the way for	prepare, make possible, lead up to
Peak	highest or maximum level or point
Plagued	trouble, annoy or torment; any widespread affliction
Precaution	taking measures in advance to avoid or avert possible harm or misfortune
Preoccupied	absorbed or engrossed to the exclusion of other things
Profoundly	showing deep insight, significance; beyond the superficial
Profuse	abundant, in great amount

R

Relapse	fall or slip back into previous state or behavior
Repercussion	result or effect of a previous event or action
Retard	slow or delay the development or progress of, hinder
Ritual	established pattern of behavior regularly performed in a set manner
Rouse	awaken, stir or incite to anger

S

Scenario	imagined sequence of events, detailed plans or possibilities
Siesta	midday or afternoon rest or nap usually taken in Latin American countries
Snort	to inhale a drug
Sobriety	state of being sober or not using alcohol
Somnolent	sleepy, drowsy, tending to cause sleep
Sorority	female social organization, usually on college campuses
Spurred	urge to action, proceed hurriedly
Stave off	keep or ward off, stall or prevent from happening
Surge	sudden strong rush or sweep; move forward or rise like a wave
Sustaining	support, hold up, endure without yielding, keep going
Symbolic	representing or pertaining to something else

T

Trance	half conscious state between sleep and waking, dazed, mentally absorbed
Trigger	anything that causes or initiates a reaction; activate

U

Unregulated	not in accord with requirements or standards

W

Watchful eye	carefully observant, alert, vigilant
Wheel and deal	highly profitable transactions by clever, crafty person

Multiple Choice Posttest

After studying the text and completing the Study Guide activities, answer these questions to determine if you need to review any areas before the course exam.

1. Daydreaming, meditation, intoxication, sleep and hypnosis are all types of _____.
   a. Self-awareness
   b. Waking consciousness
   c. Self-absorption
   d. Altered states of consciousness

2. While studying for an exam, you gradually look up from your work and begin thinking about the job and lifestyle you want after graduation. This type of thought is called _____.
   a. Auto prediction
   b. Creative thinking
   c. Meditation
   d. daydreaming

3. Our sleeping-waking cycle follows a _____ rhythm.
   a. Ultradian
   b. Monaural
   c. Diurnal
   d. Circadian

4. People may be able to adjust their biological clocks to prevent jet lag by taking small amount of the hormone _____.
   a. Serotonin
   b. Epinephrine
   c. Dopamine
   d. Melatonin

5. Which of the following is NOT seen in REM sleep?
   a. Paralysis of body muscles
   b. Periods of REM sleep get shorter as the night continues
   c. Rapid eye movement
   d. Arousal of brain activity

6. The low voltage brain waves produced during relaxes wakefulness or the twilight stage between waking and sleeping are called _____ waves.
   a. Alpha
   b. Beta
   c. Delta
   d. Theta

7. In children and young adults, periods of REM sleep get progressively ____ and periods of Stage 4 sleep get progressively _____ throughout the night.
   a. A. shorter; shorter
   b. Longer; shorter
   c. Shorter; longer
   d. Longer; shorter

8. Freud believed that sleep and dreams expressed ideas that were free from the _____.
   a. Memories of worrisome daily events
   b. Instinctive feelings of anger jealousy, or ambition
   c. Conscious controls and moral rules
   d. Case study method

9. Which of the following is NOT a suggestion to help overcome insomnia?
   a. Establish regular sleeping habits
   b. Have a strong alcoholic drink before bed
   c. Change bedtime routine
   d. Get out of bed and do something until feeling sleepy

10. Most episodes of insomnia are ____ and stem from ____.
    a. Temporary; stressful events
    b. Chronic; stressful events
    c. Temporary; underlying psychological problems
    d. Chronic; underlying psychological problems

11. Alice's strange adventures in Wonderland and Dorothy's bizarre journey through the Land of Oz most probably occurred when they were in _____ sleep.
    a. Stage 1
    b. Stage 2
    c. Stage 4
    d. REM

12. Albert is meditating. He is likely to experience each of the following EXCEPT ____.
    a. Decreased sensory awareness
    b. A sense of timelessness
    c. A sense of well-being
    d. Feelings of total relaxation

13. Some people experience alcohol as a (n) _____ because it inhibits centers in the brain that are used in higher-level thinking and inhibition of impulsive behavior.
    a. stimulant
    b. depressant
    c. hallucinogenic
    d. antigen

14. Drugs, such as heroin, that dull the senses and induce feelings of euphoria and relaxation are called _____.
    a. Hallucinogens
    b. Opiates
    c. Barbiturates
    d. Placebos

15. Chemical substances that change moods and perceptions are called _____ drugs.
    a. Psychoactive
    b. Psychedelic
    c. Psychoanalytic
    d. Psychoactive

16. In the double-blind procedure, some subjects receive a medication while the control group receives an inactive substance called _____.
    a. Control treatment
    b. Hawthorne reactor
    c. A placebo
    d. Dependent variable

17. Which of the following statements about marijuana is NOT true?
    a. Marijuana interferes with attention and short-term memory.
    b. Marijuana use can lead to cardiovascular and respiratory damage.
    c. Marijuana is the most popular drug among college students today.
    d. Marijuana users experience distortions in time perception.

18. The most common contributing factor to automobile accidents after alcohol use is ____.
    a. Other drug use
    b. Sleep deprivation
    c. Cell phone use while driving
    d. Talking to others in the car

19. Which of the following drugs can lead to psychosis similar to paranoid schizophrenia?
    a. Nicotine
    b. Marijuana
    c. Amphetamines
    d. Heroin

20. The trancelike state in which a subject responds readily to suggestions is _____.
    a. Stage 4 sleep
    b. Hypnosis
    c. Meditation
    d. coma

Answers and Explanations to Multiple Choice Posttest

1. d.   All as considered to be altered states of consciousness. p. 129

2. d.   Daydreams are apparently effortless shifts in attention away from the present into an imagined world. p. 130–1

3. d.   Circadian cycles represent the body's biological clock adapted to a 24 hour sleep/wake cycle. p. 133

4. d.   A small amount of melatonin may prevent jet lag. p. 133

5. b.   Periods of REM sleep get longer, not shorter, throughout the night. p. 135

6. a.   As measured by the EEG, low voltage alpha waves are produced during twilight sleep. p. 134

7. b.   REM sleep gets progressively longer and Stage 4 gets shorter for children and young adults. p. 135–6

8. c.   Freud believed that dreams were free from conscious control and moral rules (ego and superego). p. 139

9. b.   Alcohol interferes with getting a good night's sleep. p. 139

10. a.   Although some insomnia is part of a larger psychological problem, most insomnia is temporary and grows out of stressful events. p 138

11. d.   Most graphic dreams are reported to occur in REM sleep. p. 138

12. a.   Regular meditators report increased sensory awareness, timelessness, well-being and total relaxation. p. 159

13. a.   Alcohol may be experienced as a stimulant because it decreases our inhibitions. p. 150

14. b.   Heroin is an opiate. p. 150

15. d.   Psychoactive drugs are chemical substances that alter moods and perceptions. p. 142

16. c.   A placebo is an inactive substance given to the control group. p. 144

17. c.   Marijuana, the most popularly used illegal drug in the U.S., is only the fourth most popular drug among students after alcohol, caffeine and nicotine. p. 155

18. b.   Driving while sleepy is just as dangerous as driving while drunk. p. 136

19. c.   Chronic users may develop amphetamine psychosis which resembles paranoid schizophrenia. p. 153

20. b.   Hypnosis is a trancelike state in which a person responds readily to suggestions. p. 160

Key Vocabulary Terms

Cut out each term and use as study cards.
Definition is on the back side of each term.

Consciousness	Non-REM (NREM) sleep
Waking consciousness	Dreams
Altered state of consciousness	Insomnia
Daydreaming	Narcolepsy
REM (paradoxical) sleep	Conscious Experience

Non-rapid-eye-movement stages of sleep that alternate with REM stages during the sleep cycle.

Our awareness of various cognitive processes, such as sleeping, dreaming, concentrating, and making decisions.

Vivid visual and auditory experiences that occur primarily during REM periods of sleep.

Mental state that encompasses the thoughts, feelings, and perceptions that occur when we are awake and reasonably alert.

Sleep disorder characterized by difficulty in falling asleep or remaining asleep throughout the night.

Mental state that differs noticeably from normal waking consciousness.

Hereditary sleep disorder characterized by sudden nodding off during the day and sudden loss of muscle tone following moments of emotional excitement.

Apparently effortless shifts in attention away from the here and now into a private world of make believe.

Selection of the most important information to attend to and filtering out competing stimuli.

Sleep stage characterized by rapid eye movement and increased dreaming.

Meditation	Drug altered consciousness
Hypnosis	Apnea
Psychoactive drugs	Double-blind procedure
Substance abuse	Placebo
Substance dependence	Depressants

The use of psychoactive drugs to alter waking consciousness.

Any of various methods of concentration, reflection, or focusing of thoughts undertaken to suppress the activity of the sympathetic nervous system.

Sleep disorder characterized by breathing difficulty during the night and exhaustion during the day.

Trancelike state in which the subject responds readily to suggestions.

Experiment in which neither the subject nor the researcher know which subjects are receiving the treatment.

Chemical substances that change moods and perceptions.

Chemically inactive substance used for comparison with active drugs in experiments on the effects of drugs.

A pattern of drug use that diminishes the user's ability to fulfill responsibilities; that results in repeated use of a drug in dangerous situations, or leads to legal problems.

Chemicals that slow down behavior or cognitive processes.

A pattern of compulsive drug taking that results in tolerance, withdrawal or other specific symptoms.

Alcohol	Cocaine
Barbiturates	Hallucinogens
Opiates	LSD
Stimulants	Marijuana
Amphetamines	Hypnotic suggestion

Drug derived from cocoa plant that produces sense of euphoria by stimulating the sympathetic nervous system, also produces anxiety, depression and addictive cravings.

Depressant that is the intoxicating ingredient in whiskey, beer, wine, and other fermented or distilled liquors.

Any of a number of drugs, such as LSD and mescaline, that distort visual and auditory perception.

Potentially deadly depressants, first used for their sedative and anticonvulsant properties, now used only to treat such conditions as epilepsy and arthritis.

Hallucinogen or "psychedelic" drug that produces hallucinations and delusions similar to those occurring in a psychotic state.

Drugs, such as opium and heroin, derived from opium poppy, dull senses, induce feelings of euphoria, and relaxation. Synthetic drugs resembling opium derivatives.

A mild hallucinogen that produces a "high," feelings of euphoria, a sense of well-being, and swings in mood from gaiety to relaxation and may cause anxiety and paranoia.

Drugs, including amphetamines, and cocaine, that stimulate the sympathetic nervous system and produce feelings of optimism and boundless energy.

A measure of an individual's susceptibility to hypnosis.

Stimulant drugs that initially produce "rushes" of euphoria often followed by sudden "crashes" and, sometimes, severe depression.

5 Learning

Use this section for class and text notes. Distinguish between lecture notes, textbook concepts, topics emphasized on the exams and your own comments.

Learning

1. Classical Conditioning   page 165

    A. Pavlov's Conditioning Experiments

    B. Elements of Classical Conditioning

        • Unconditioned stimulus (US)

        • Unconditioned response (UR)

        • Conditioned stimulus (CS)

        • Conditioned response (CR)

    C. Establishing a Classically Conditioned Response

    D. Classical Conditioning in Humans

        • Desensitization therapy

        • Classical Conditioning and the Immune System

    E. Classical Conditioning is Selective

        • Preparedness

        • Conditioned taste aversion

2. Operant Conditioning   page 170

   A. Elements of Operant Conditioning

      • Emitted behaviors

      • Operant behaviors

      • Reinforcers

      • Punishers

      • Law of Effect

      • Principle of reinforcement

      • What is Punishment?

   B. Establishing an Operantly Conditioned Response

      • Skinner box

      • Shaping

UNDERSTANDING Ourselves   page 174

Modifying Your Own Behavior

   C. A Closer Look at Reinforcement

   • Negative reinforcers

   • Shaping Behavioral Change Through Biofeedback

      – Biofeedback

   D. A Closer Look at Punishment

      • Punishment

      • Avoidance Training

   E. Learned Helplessness

4.   Cognitive Learning   page 188

 A. Latent Learning and Cognitive Maps

  • Latent Learning

  • Cognitive Maps

 B. Insight and Learning Sets

  • Insight

  • Learning set

  • Human Insight

 C. Learning by Observing

  • Observational or vicarious learning

  • Social learning theorists

  • Vicarious reinforcement or vicarious punishment

Learning Objectives and Questions

After you have read and studied this chapter, you should be able to complete the following statements. Your exam is written based on these learning objectives.

LEARNING OBJECTIVES

1. Describe the results of Pavlov's classical conditioning studies in terms of the US, UR, CS, CR by describing his famous salivation/dog study.

2. Discuss the development and success of desensitization therapy and how classical conditioning principles apply to human life.

3. Describe the principles of reinforcement by defining primary reinforcers and secondary reinforcers and provide and example of each.

4. Compare and contrast positive reinforcement and negative reinforcement in terms of their methods and effects.

5. Name and briefly discuss the four schedules of reinforcement and provide an example for each schedule and the resulting pattern of behavior for each schedule. Explain the effects of delay of reinforcement.

6. Discuss the requirements for punishment to be effective as well as the dangers and limitations of using punishment to change behavior. Describe the role of avoidance training in using punishment to change behavior.

7. Explain the concepts of preparedness. Summarize research findings on food aversion and how it relates to preparedness.

8. Explain learned helplessness and describe how it developed. Discuss what effects it has on people and animals once established.

9. Briefly discuss the focus of cognitive learning theorists and describe some representative research to support their views.

10. Discuss social learning theory and its implications for human learning.

ESSAY QUESTIONS

11. Explain Watson's goals and the results of his work with Little Albert. Provide a personal example of classical conditioning in your learning experience.

12. Explain the processes of extinction, spontaneous recovery, shaping, inhibition, stimulus generalization, discrimination and higher-order conditioning.

13. Compare and contrast classical conditioning with operant conditioning. Discuss which theory appears to explain MOST behavior, and why.

14. Discuss the phenomenon of insight learning and whether it is only applicable for humans.

15. Explain the steps involved in modifying your own behavior.

16. Discuss the process of shaping behavioral change through biofeedback and its popularity and criticism in the research and medical communities.

17. Compare the importance of contingencies in classical and operant conditioning. Discuss backward conditioning and blocking.

Language Support

Students identified the following words from the text as needing more explanation. This page can be cut-out, folded in half, and used as a bookmark for this chapter.

A

Accidentally	happening unexpectedly or by chance
Anecdotal	based on incidental observations or reports rather than systematic evaluation
Abstract	thought apart from concrete reality or actuality; not applied or practical; theoretical; difficult to understand
Alleviate	get rid of or make less, stop
Attribute	state the cause of; consider resulting from a specific cause, a quality or characteristic

B

Bully	to intimidate or terrorize; an overbearing person who picks on those smaller or weaker

C

Congested	overcrowded; overburdened; stuffed up
Consistent	in agreement with; constantly adhering to the same form or principles
Clue in	provide with necessary information
Caliber	degree or level of competence or capacity
Contingent	dependent on chance or fulfilling a condition; uncertainty
Coincidence	mere chance of 2 or more events taking place at one time
"The coast is clear"	nothing is present to impede or endanger one's progress; proceed
Crucial	of vital or critical importance to an outcome or decision
Casino	large room or building used for professional gambling
Chore	small routine or task
Convert	change something into a different form or property or use for another purpose
Confine	enclose within boundaries or limits; restrict
Concrete	actual things or realities unlike abstractions, solid form

D

Devise	to form a plan; create from existing ideas or concepts
Diminishing	returns less improvement or benefit over time; any increase fails to occur
Drool	to water at the mouth in anticipation of food; salivate
Dysfunction	impaired functioning as in a body organ or social system
Discontinue	cease to use or produce, terminate, stop
Downplay	represent as unimportant or insignificant; minimize
Drawback	undesirable or objectionable feature; disadvantage

E

Entail	involve or cause by necessity or as a consequence of
Eventually	at some later time; finally
Extensive	comprehensive, far-reaching, thorough
Encourage	stimulate, approve, foster, inspire, promote, motivate
Elapse	passage of time

F

Fade	to lose strength or dim, disappear or die gradually
First-hand	directly from the original source
Fine-tune	make adjustments to produce improvement or stability

G

Gauge	estimate, judge, conform to a standard, delineate

H

Harsh	unpleasant, severe, uncomfortable
Hurdle	barrier, difficulty to overcome, obstacle
Half-hearted	having or showing little or no enthusiasm
Hard-wired	a built in or intrinsic behavior pattern that is difficult to change
Horror	shocking, strong aversion, overwhelming, terrifying fear

I

Impede	obstacles or hindrances that retard the movement or progress of an event
Indifferent	apathetic; with little interest or concern; having no bias or preference; neutral
Inquiry	an investigation that seeks truth, conformation or knowledge; question or ask
Insightful	instant grasping of the true nature of something through intuitive understanding
Incontinence	inability to restrain or control (i.e., elimination); lacking moderation
Isolate	set or place apart or detach from others
Implication	shown to be involved, to imply or suggest
Inadvertently	unintentional, lack of attention
IRS	Internal Revenue Service
Impose	to establish by authority; to push on others
Infraction	violation, breach or break a law or commitment
Imitate	copy, follow a model, mimic, impersonate
Inclination	preference or tendency towards, a leaning

J

Jackpot	chief prize in a game or contest; an outstanding success

L

Listless	having no interest, spiritless
Likelihood	probability or change of something happening
Legitimate	according to the law, established rules and principles, authorized
Lisp	defect in speech with s and z pronounced like the th-sound

M

Mallet	hammer-like tool with enlarged head used for repair, music or games
Maintain	keep a certain way, continue, preserve
Misbehave	improper conduct
Misdeed	an immoral act
Marathon	an extended contest or event requiring great endurance

N

Noxious	harmful to health or well being, toxic; corrupting influence
NASA	National Aeronautics and Space Administration
Nausea	sick to stomach usually regarding food and often resulting in vomiting

O

Overwhelmed	overpowered in mind or feelings; excessively burdened
Overtly	open to view or knowledge; not secret or hidden
Onset	beginning or start; assault or attack

P

Persistent	enduring or lasting, constantly repeated, continuing or permanent
Pastime	something that makes time pass enjoyably such as a hobby or sport
Privilege	special right or benefit, entitlement or advantage
Pop up	something that springs up or out, often unexpectedly
Potentially	capable of becoming; possibility; latent excellence or ability that is undeveloped

Q

Quackery — fraudulent methods or practices; claiming qualifications that are lacking; a phony

R

Reckless — unconcerned about consequences; careless

Revulsion — strong feelings of dislike or disgust

Rigorous — rigid, severe, exact, precise, logically valid

Rerun — watching film or show again; restating something; rehash

Rude — discourteous, without refinement, impolite

S

Scold — find fault with; use loud and abusive speech

Subsequent — occurring or coming later; following in order

Significant — having importance

Successive — following in order or in an uninterrupted sequence

Strategy — plan or method for achieving a specific goal

Spotlight — intense light focused to pick out something

Strut — walk with strong bearing, chest pushed out

Swift — move with great speed or velocity, happening quickly without delay, quick to act

Signal — an act or event that causes an action; indication or warning

Slot machine — gambling or vending machine operating by inserting money

Scary — frightening or alarming; filling with fear or worry

Sparingly — economically, provided in small amounts, meager or frugal

Stamped in — to record, impress or imprint

Spanking — strike with open hand, blow, slap, punishment

T

Tedious — tiresome, wordy

Temptation — enticed to do something considered wrong; to appeal strongly

U

Ultimately — highest, most desirable, fundamental or basic, the outcome

Undergo — to endure, to be subjected to, sustain

Up to date — keep up with the times in accordance with the latest or newest trends

Undermine — impair, weaken, destroy by subtle stages

V

Venture — undertaking involving risk or uncertainty, expose to hazard or risk

Virtually — for the most part; almost totally; just about

Vicious — spiteful, unpleasantly intense, savage, malicious

Victory — triumph; success or superior position achieved against an opponent

W

Withhold — hold back; refrain from giving

Z

Zero gravity — condition in which the apparent effect of gravity is zero; freefalling or in orbit

After studying the text and completing the Study Guide activities, answer these questions to determine if you need to review any areas before the course exam.

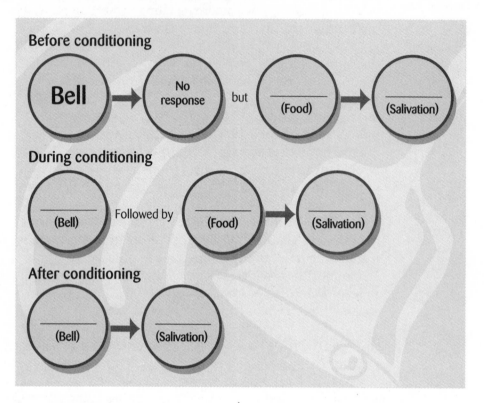

Before conditioning

Bell → No response   but   _____ (Food) → _____ (Salivation)

During conditioning

_____ (Bell)   Followed by   _____ (Food) → _____ (Salivation)

After conditioning

_____ (Bell) → _____ (Salivation)

1. In the chart above, provide the correct elements in the 3 stages of Pavlov's classical conditioning experiment.
   a. Conditioned response (CR)
   b. Unconditioned stimulus (US)
   c. Conditioned stimulus (CS)
   d. Unconditioned response (UR)

2. In Watson's experiment with Little Albert, the conditioned response (CR) was _____.
   a. fear of the experimenter (Watson)
   b. fear of the laboratory
   c. fear of the rat
   d. fear of the loud noise

3. The idea that a behavior will increase or decrease based on the consequences that follow the behavior is crucial to ____.
   a. operant conditioning
   b. vicarious learning
   c. classical conditioning
   d. insight learning

4. In classical conditioning the learner is ____, and in operant conditioning the learner is _____.
   a. passive; passive
   b. passive; active
   c. active; passive
   d. active; active

5. Any stimulus that follows a behavior and increases the likelihood that the behavior will be repeated is called a _____.
   a. cue
   b. situational stimulus
   c. reinforcer
   d. higher-order conditioner

6. Any stimulus that follows a behavior and decreases the likelihood that the behavior will be repeated is called a _____.
   a. cue
   b. situational stimulus
   c. reinforcer
   d. punisher

7. Changing behavior through the reinforcement of partial responses is called _____.
   a. modeling
   b. shaping
   c. negative reinforcement
   d. classical conditioning

8. _____ therapy for treating anxiety involves the pairing of relaxation training with systematic exposure to the fearful stimulus.
   a. Operant conditioning
   b. Shaping
   c. Aversive conditioning
   d. Desensitization

9. The process of learning is defined as experience resulting in _____.
   a. amplification of sensory stimuli
   b. delayed genetic behavioral contributions
   c. relatively permanent behavior change
   d. acquisition of motivation

10. A dolphin learns to swim toward a blue platform but not toward a platform of a different color. This shows the concept of _____.
    a. discrimination
    b. modeling
    c. higher-order conditioning
    d. stimulus generalization

11. Reacting to a stimulus that is similar to one that you have already learned to react to is called _____.
    a. response generalization
    b. modeling
    c. higher-order conditioning
    d. stimulus generalization

12. Failure to take steps to avoid or escape from an unpleasant or aversive stimulus that occurs as a result of previous exposure to unavoidable painful stimuli is called _____.
    a. learned helplessness
    b. avoidance learning
    c. aversive conditioning
    d. vicarious learning

13. The process in which a learned response, which has been extinguished suddenly, reappears on its own, with no retraining is called _____.
    a. reaction formation
    b. generalization
    c. spontaneous recovery
    d. shaping

14. A reinforcer that is reinforcing in and of itself is called a _____ and a reinforcer that takes on reinforcing properties only through association with other reinforcers is called a (n) _____ reinforcer.
    a. direct reinforcer/indirect reinforcer
    b. delayed reinforcer/immediate reinforcer
    c. primary reinforcer/secondary reinforcer
    d. secondary reinforcer/primary reinforcer

15. The idea that learning occurs and is stored up, even when behaviors are not reinforced is called _____.
    a. insight
    b. latent learning
    c. placebo learning
    d. innate learning

16. The type of learning that involves elements suddenly coming together so that the solution to a problem is clear is called _____.
    a. latent learning
    b. insight
    c. cognitive mapping
    d. vicarious learning

17. The mental picture of an area, such as a floor plan of a building is called _____.
    a. a perceptual illusion
    b. a mental set
    c. subliminal perception
    d. a cognitive map

18. Becoming increasingly more effective in solving problems as one experiences solving problems is called _____.
    a. a learning set
    b. a response cue
    c. latent learning
    d. a response set

19. An operant conditioning technique in which a learner gains control over some biological response is _____.
    a. contingency training
    b. preparedness
    c. social learning
    d. biofeedback

20. Which of the following steps is the basic principle of self-modification of behavior?
    a. Decide what behavior you want to acquire.
    b. Define the target behavior precisely
    c Monitor your present behavior.
    d. Provide yourself with a positive reinforcer that is contingent upon specific improvements in the target behavior.

21. Match the correct example with the type of schedule of reinforcement shown on the chart below.
    a. Scott gets paid a salary every two weeks.
    b. Having unannounced psychology pop quizzes.
    c. Getting paid a commission for every car sold.
    d. Payoff from a Las Vegas slot machine.

Answers and Explanations to Multiple Choice Posttest

1. Before conditioning: B (Food is the unlearned or unconditioned stimulus(US)

   D (Salivation is the unlearned or unconditioned response (UR) to food (S)

   During conditioning: C (Bell is the learned or conditioned stimulus when paired with food (US); B (Food is the US); A (Salivation becomes a learned response (CR) when paired with the bell and food)

   After conditioning: C (Bell is the learned or conditioned stimulus (CS); A (Salivation is the learned or conditioned response (CR) to the bell (CS). p. 167, Fig. 5.2

2. c. Albert was conditioned (learned) to fear the rat (CS) because it was paired with a loud noise (US). p. 16

3. a. Operant conditioning is designed on the principle of acting in a way to gain something desired or avoiding something unpleasant. p. 171

4. b. Classical conditioning is passive; operant conditioning is active. p. 171

5. c. Reinforcers increase behavior. p. 171

6. d. Punishment decreases the behavior. p. 171

7. b. Shaping is the process of changing behavior by reinforcing partial responses or successive approximations. p. 173

8. d. Desensitization is a conditioning technique designed to gradually reduce anxiety about a situation or object. p. 168

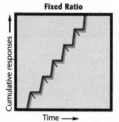

Fixed Ratio

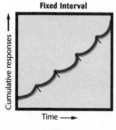

Fixed Interval

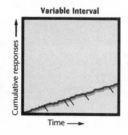

Variable Interval

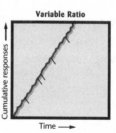

Variable Ratio

_____   _____   _____   _____

9. c. Learning is the process by which experience or practice results in a relatively permanent change in behavior or potential behavior. p. 165

10. a. Stimulus discrimination is learning to respond only to one stimulus and inhibit the response to all other stimuli. p. 186

11. d. Reacting to another stimulus is called stimulus generalization. p. 186

12. a. Learned helplessness is the failure to takes steps to avoid or escape an unpleasant or aversive stimulus. p. 178

13. c. Spontaneous recovery is the reappearance of an extinguished response after with passage of time, without training. p. 184

14. c. Primary reinforcers (food) are reinforcing in and of themselves and secondary reinforcers are learned through association with other reinforcers (money). p. 187

15. b. Latent learning is not immediately reflected in a behavior change. p. 189

16. b. Insight is a sudden solution to a problem. p. 190

17. d. A learned mental picture of a spatial environment is a cognitive map. p. 189

18. a. A learning set enables us to learn more effectively with experience. p. 191.

19. d. Biofeedback consists of learning control over a biological response. p. 175

20. d. Positive reinforcers as well as consequences for your behavior are the basic principles of self-modification of behavior. p. 174

21. a. B Fixed interval (FI)
    b. D Variable interval (VI)
    c. A Fixed ratio (FR)
    d. C Variable ratio (VR) pp. 181–3

Key Vocabulary Terms

Cut out each term and use as study cards.
Definition is on the back side of each term.

Learning	Unconditioned response (UR)
Conditioning	Conditioned stimulus (CS)
Classical or Pavlovian conditioning	Conditioned response (CR)
Operant or instrumental conditioning	Desensitization therapy
Unconditioned stimulus (US)	Conditioned taste aversion

Response that takes place in an organism whenever an unconditioned stimulus occurs.	The process by which experience or practice results in a relatively permanent change in behavior or potential behavior.
Originally neutral stimulus that is paired with an unconditioned stimulus and eventually produces the desired response in an organism when presented alone.	The acquisition of specific patterns of behavior in the presence of well-defined stimuli.
After conditioning, the response an organism produces when a conditioned stimulus is presented.	Type of learning in which a response naturally elicited by one stimulus comes to be elicited by a different, formerly neutral stimulus.
Conditioning technique designed to gradually reduce anxiety about a particular object or situation.	Type of learning in which behaviors are emitted (in the presence of specific stimuli) to earn rewards or avoid punishments.
Conditioned avoidance of certain foods even if there is only one pairing of conditioned and unconditioned stimuli.	Stimulus that invariably causes an organism to respond in a specific way.

Operant behavior	Negative reinforcer
Reinforcer	Punishment
Punishers	Avoidance training
Law of effect (principle of reinforcement)	Learned helplessness
Positive reinforcer	Intermittent pairing

Any event whose reduction or termination increases the likelihood that ongoing behavior will recur.

Behavior designed to operate on the environment in a way that will gain something desired or avoid something unpleasant.

Any event whose presence decreases the likelihood that ongoing behavior will recur.

A stimulus that follows a behavior and increases the likelihood that the behavior will be repeated.

Learning a desirable behavior to prevent the occurrence of something unpleasant, such as punishment.

A stimulus that follows a behavior and decreases the likelihood that the behavior will be repeated.

Failure to take steps to avoid or escape from an unpleasant or aversive stimulus that occurs as a result of previous exposure to unavoidable painful stimuli.

Thorndike's theory that behavior consistently rewarded will be "stamped in " as learned behavior and behavior that brings about discomfort will be stamped out.

Pairing the conditioned stimulus and the unconditioned stimulus on only a portion of the learning trials.

Any event whose presence increases the likelihood that ongoing behavior will recur.

Skinner box	Stimulus discrimination
Shaping	Response generalization
Extinction	Higher-order conditioning
Spontaneous recovery	Primary reinforcer
Stimulus generalization	Secondary reinforcer

Learning to respond to only one stimulus and to inhibit the response to all other stimuli.

Box often used in operant conditioning of animals; it limits the available response and thus increases the likelihood that the desired response will occur.

Giving a response that is somewhat different from the response originally learned to that stimulus.

Reinforcing successive approximations to a desired behavior.

Conditioning based on previous learning; the conditioned stimulus serves as an unconditioned stimulus for further training.

Decrease in the strength or frequency, or stopping of a learned response due to failure to continue pairing the US and CS (classical conditioning) or the withholding of reinforcement (operant conditioning).

Reinforcer that is rewarding in itself, such as food, water, and sex.

The reappearance of an extinguished response after the passage of time, without training.

Reinforcer whose value is acquired through association with other primary or secondary reinforcers.

Tendency to respond to cues that are similar to the original learning.

Contingency	Fixed-ratio schedule
Blocking	Variable-ratio schedule
Schedule of reinforcement	Biofeedback
Fixed-interval schedule	Cognitive learning
Variable-interval schedule	Latent learning

Reinforcement schedule in which the correct response is reinforced after a fixed number of correct responses.

A reliable "if-then" relationship between two events such as a CS and a US.

Reinforcement schedule in which a varying number of correct responses must occur before reinforcement is presented.

Process whereby prior conditioning prevents conditioning to a second stimulus even when the two stimuli are presented simultaneously.

A technique that uses monitoring devices to provide precise information about internal physiological processes, such as heart rate or blood pressure, to teach people to gain voluntary control over these functions.

In operant conditioning, the rule for determining when and how often reinforcers will be delivered.

Learning that depends on mental processes that are not directly observable.

Reinforcement schedule that calls for reinforcement of a correct response after a fixed length of time since the last reinforcement.

Learning that is not immediately reflected in a behavior change.

Reinforcement schedule in which a correct response is reinforced after varying lengths of time following the last reinforcement.

Cognitive map	Vicarious reinforcement/ punishment
Insight	Preparedness
Learning set	Stimulus control
Social learning theorists	
Observational (or vicarious) learning	

The extent to which we imitate behaviors learned through observation that is modified by watching others who are reinforced or punished for their behavior.	A learned mental image of a spatial environment that may be called on to solve problems when stimuli in the environment change.
A biological readiness to learn certain associations because of their survival advantages.	Learning that occurs rapidly as a result of understanding all the elements of a problem.
Occurs when conditioned responses are influenced by surrounding cues in the environment.	Ability to become increasingly more effective in solving problems as more problems are solved.
	Psychologists whose view of learning emphasizes the ability to learn by observing a model or receiving instructions, without firsthand experience by the learner.
	Learning by observing other people's behavior.

6

Memory

Use this section for class and text notes. Distinguish between lecture notes, textbook concepts, topics emphasized on the exams and your own comments.

Memory

Information Processing Model

1. The Sensory Registers   page 202

    A. Visual and Auditory Registers

    B. Attention

2. Short-Term Memory   page 205

    A. Chunking

    B. Encoding in STM

    C. Maintaining in STM

    D. Rote Rehearsal (maintenance rehearsal)

3. Long-Term Memory   page 207

    A. Capacity of LTM

    B. Encoding in LTM

C. Serial Position Effect

D. Maintaining LTM

- Rote Rehearsal

- Elaborative Rehearsal

- Schemata

E. Types of LTM

- Episodic Memory

- Semantic Memory

- Procedural Memory

- Emotional Memory

F. Explicit and Implicit Memory

- Explicit Memory

- Implicit Memory

---

4. The Biology of Memory   page 213

A. How are memories stored?

B. Where are memories stored?

---

5. Forgetting   page 216

A. The Biology of Forgetting

B. Experience and Forgetting

- Interference

    - retroactive interference

    - proactive interference

- Situational Factors

    - context-dependent memory

    - state-dependent memory

- The Reconstructive Process

UNDERSTANDING the World Around Us   page 218

Eyewitness Testimony: Can We Trust It?

C. Improving Your Memory

1. Develop motivation.

2. Practice memory skills.

3. Be confident in your ability to remember.

4. Minimize distractions.

5. Stay focused.

6. Make connections between new material and other information already stored in your long-term memory.

   - Mnemonics

7. Use mental imagery.

8. Use retrieval cues.

9. Rely on more than memory alone.

10. Be aware that your own personal schemata may distort your recall of events.

---

6.   Special Topics in Memory   page 221

A. Cultural influences

B. Autobiographical memory

C. Childhood amnesia

D. Flashbulb memories

E. Recovered Memories

UNDERSTANDING Ourselves   page 222

Improving Your Memory for Textbook Material

SQRRR or SQ3R Method

1. Survey

2. Question

3. Read

4. Recite

5. Review

Learning Objectives and Questions

After you have read and studied this chapter, you should be able to complete the following statements. Your exam is written based on these learning objectives.

LEARNING OBJECTIVES

1. Describe the purpose, capacity and function of the sensory register including the differences between the visual and auditory registers.

2. Learn about the purpose, capacity and function of short-term and long-term memory and discuss their similarities and differences.

3. Describe how information is coded in short-term memory and discuss how decay and interference play a role in recalling information from short-term memory.

4. Compare and contrast rote rehearsal with elaborative rehearsal. Give examples of when each is most effectively utilized. Discuss retrograde amnesia and how it relates to rote and elaborative rehearsal.

5. Define schemata and discuss how our schemata may affect what we recall and how it may help to fill in missing information.

6. Define and discuss semantic, procedural, episodic and emotional memory giving an example for each.

7. Compare and contrast explicit and implicit memories and comment upon the implications of implicit memory for everyday life.

8. Discuss how information is coded in long-term memory and how decay, interference and retrieval cues play a part in recalling information from long-term memory.

9. Discuss Freud's theory of repressed memories and relate this to the concept of recovered memories.

10. Define autobiographical and flashbulb memories and discuss the accuracy of these kind of memories and what kinds of early memories people may be more likely to have.

11. Learn the 10 steps for improving your memory in school.

12. Define mnemonics, describe at least 3 mnemonic devices and discuss their effectiveness.

13. Identify each step in the SQ3R method and explain how each step works.

14. Summarize the research on the biological basis of memory. Know the major brain structures and regions involved in memory and the role of neurotransmitters in storage or loss of memory.

15. Discuss Korsakoff's syndrome and Alzheimer's disease; their causes and effects on brain damage and memory loss.

ESSAY QUESTIONS

1. Explain Broadbent's filter theory and Treisman's modified filter theory. Which theory best accounts for how people select what they attend to from the massive amount of information entering the sensory register?

2. Define proactive and retroactive interference. Describe reconstructive memory and give two examples of how we utilize it in real-life situations.

3. Discuss the research on the reliability of eyewitness testimony and how this relates to recovered memories. What do scientists currently believe about the accuracy and reliability of recovered memories?

4. Recall your memories of the incidents surrounding September 11th as they relate to the definition of a flashbulb memory. Discuss the events surrounding your learning of the event; the emotions and thoughts you experienced then and how this event has affected your present life.

5. Make a commitment to yourself to use at least 3 steps for improving your memory. List them here and describe how you will make them new habits.

Language Support

Students identified the following words from the text as needing more explanation. This page can be cut-out, folded in half, and used as a bookmark for this chapter.

A

Absentminded	preoccupied with one's thoughts and unaware or forgetful of other matters
Acoustically	related to sound or hearing
Acrostics	written words in which the 1st, last or other letters form a word or phrase
Amnesic	complete or partial loss of a large block of interrelated memories due to brain injury or shock
Anagram	word, phrase or sentence formed from another by rearranging its letters
Analogous	corresponding to or similar in some way
Arbitrary	without restriction or special value, uncertain, dependent on one's judgment or will
Articulate	expressing self readily, clearly or effectively, intelligible, well spoken
Ascribe	credit or attribute, think of as belonging to a quality or characteristic

B

Barring	keeping out, excluding by exception, to legally object

C

Capture	hold the interest or record in a permanent file, preserve, represent, emphasize
Cluster	group together a number of similar items
Coherent	understandable, having clarity and consistency
Concussion	jarring injury to brain from a sharp blow to the head resulting in disturbed cerebral function
Conspicuous	obvious, easily seen, readily observable, attracting attention
Contention	discord; rivalry or competition
Corroborate	to support with evidence or authority, making more certain, confirm

D

Deed	performance, accomplishment or action
Descent	passing from higher or lower state or degree; ancestry or lineage
Disoriented	loss of bearing, sense of time, place, identify, confused, displaced
Dispersed	move apart in different directions; spread widely
Doggedly	marked by stubborn determination; holding on; not giving up
Durability	capable of lasting or enduring; highly resistant to wear or decay

E

Effortlessly	requiring little or no effort
Elude	avoid; unable to perceive or understand
Enormity	of momentous importance; considerable departure from the unexpected
Exception	excluding; rare instance not conforming to general rule
Extraordinary	going beyond the usual, regular or customary

F

Fanatic	person with extreme enthusiasm or zeal
Fleeting	vanishing or passing quickly
Forge	move ahead with increased speed and effectiveness, progress steadily

G

Going through the motions	seeming to take the appropriate actions

I

Inadequate	insufficient; having a shortcoming or deficiency
Inadvertently	happen by accident, unintentional, not focusing the mind on a matter
Incapable	lacking the capacity or qualification for the purpose, unfit
Indistinguishable	not clearly seen or understood; differences too subtle to be made
Integral	essential part of the whole; necessary for completion
Interrupt	cut off or stop before completion, break continuity or uniformity
Invariably	incapable of being changed, static, constant
Intact	unaltered or unbroken, complete or whole

J

Jingle	short, catchy succession of repetitive sounds, song
Jot	to write down quickly; least amount or briefly; a little bit
Jumble	mentally confused, disordered

L

Larcenous	theft, robbery; wrongful taking of another's goods
Lineage	one's derivation from; common ancestry of a group

M

Mingle	unite, form or mix, blend together
Myriad	innumerable or great number of people, things, variations or aspects

N

Nazi	member of Hitler's political party who controlled Germany from 1933-45, advocated Aryan (white) supremacy, leading to World War II and the Holocaust

O

Oblivious	lacking active, conscious knowledge, awareness or memory of
Odd	different from usual or expected; bizarre; remaining after all are paired
Orator	speaker with great eloquence using appropriate, effective language
Over-learning	continue to study or practice after attaining advanced knowledge or skill

P

Password	secret word or expression used to gain access to restricted information
Pivotal	crucial; vitally important; turning point
Plausible	appearing to be true, reasonable, believable or credible
Podium	lectern; stand for speaker's notes or books
Prodigious	extraordinary degree, amount or quality; exceeding usual bounds or accepted beliefs
Prompt	without delay; to assist by suggesting, inspiring, reminding
Pronounced	strongly marked; noticeable; free from doubt or wavering

R

Rambling	moving aimlessly; speaking in wandering, long-winded fashion
Recast	rearrange, remodel or reconstruct
Refresh	stimulate the memory, revive or renew the vigor or energy of
Relevance	related to the matter; ability to retrieve material needed
Rely	depend upon; have confidence based on experience
Reminiscence	recall to mind long forgotten experiences or facts; think about past memories

S

Sabotage	action or procedure that deliberately hurts or defeats
Scramble	to move, collect or organize things in a hurried, disorganized manner
Secluded	isolate or remove from social contact or activity
Senseless	lacking meaning, foolish, making no sense
Sequence	one thing after another, a continuously connected series
Similarly	having common characteristics; closely resembling

Simultaneously	existing or occurring at the same time; coincidence
Storehouse	place where large supply of facts, knowledge or other material is store
T	
Translate	move or change form one state or form to another (i.e., language)
Trivia	unimportant matters, facts or details; quiz game involving obscure facts
U	
Unreliable	not giving the same results on successive trials; can't count on
V	
Verbatim	using the exact same words; word for word

Multiple Choice Posttest

After studying the text and completing the Study Guide activities, answer these questions to determine if you need to review any areas before the course exam.

1. Label the elements of the information processing model of memory illustrated in Figure 6-1 on page 203. Select from the following terms: a) decay; b) repetition; c) attention; d)sensory register; e) retrieval; f)interference; g) rehearsal; h) long-term memory; i) coding; j) short term memory; k) external stimulus.

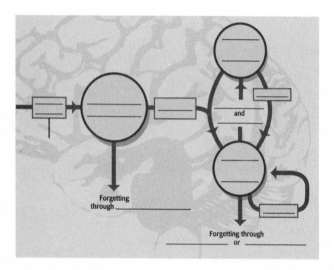

2. Our visual impression of our friend walking past us would initially be found in the _____.
   a. sensory registers
   b. short-term memory
   c. long-term memory
   d. hippocampus

3. What we are thinking of at any given moment, or what we commonly know as "consciousness," is _____.
   a. long-term memory
   b. Short-term memory
   c. secondary memory
   d. sensory registers

4. Information is grouped for storage in short-term memory through the process of _____.
   a. categorizing
   b. chunking
   c. rote rehearsal
   d. nonsense syllables

5. The linking of new information in short-term memory to familiar material stored in long-term memory is called _____.
   a. elaborative rehearsal
   b. rote rehearsal
   c. semantic rehearsal
   d. chunking

6. The inability to recall events immediately preceding an accident or injury, but without loss of earlier memory is called _____ amnesia.
   a. psychogenic
   b. retroactive
   c. retrograde
   d. fugue

7. The portion of long-term memory that stores general facts and information is called _____.
   a. eidetic
   b. episodic
   c. semantic
   d. procedural

8. While memorizing a list of words, students were exposed to the scent of chocolate. If the students recall more words when there is the scent of chocolate present, then the effect of chocolate is most likely due to _____ memory.
   a. explicit
   b. implicit
   c. procedural
   d. eidetic

9. Proactive interference of long-term memory means that _____.
   a. Old material has eliminated memories of new material
   b. Old material interferes with remembering new material
   c. New material represses short-term memories
   d. New material interferes with remembering old material

10. When memories are not lost but are transformed into something somewhat different, it is called _____.
    a. Retroactive interference
    b. Eidetic memory
    c. Proactive interference
    d. Reconstructive memory

11. The phenomenon whereby most people cannot recall events that occurred in their life before the age of 2, is called _____.
    a. Infantile autism
    b. Psychogenic amnesia
    c. fugue amnesia
    d. childhood amnesia

12. Our recollection of events that occurred in our life and when those events took place is called _____ memory.
    a. Autobiographical
    b. Reconstructive
    c. Semantic
    d. Procedural

13. Memories that concern highly significant events and are vividly remembered, such as the World Trade Center and Pentagon events of September 11th, 2001, are called _____.
    a. Eyewitness images
    b. Flashbulb memories
    c. now print images
    d. photographic memories

14. The most important determinant of interference is _____.
    a. Similarity of material
    b. Complexity of material
    c. Decay
    d. Rehearsal time

15. Remembering a telephone number because it contains the numbers of the year in which you were born is an example of the use of _____.
    a. A mnemonic device
    b. Association
    c. eidetic imagery
    d. chunking

16. The hippocampus is important for _____.
    a. Transferring information from short-term to long-term memory
    b. The retrieval of memories from long-term memory
    c. maintaining a constant level of attention
    d. the formation of short-term memory

17. The neurotransmitter that appears to be instrumental in the memory process is _____.
    a. Serotonin
    b. Dopamine
    c. norepinephrine
    d. acetylcholine

18. In more than 1,000 cases in which innocent people were wrongly convicted of a crime, the single most pervasive element leading to the wrongful conviction was _____.
    a. Faulty forensic work by police labs
    b. Phony evidence "planted" by the police
    c. Faulty eyewitness testimony
    d. Misinterpretations of the law by judges and juries

19. Each of the following is a recommended strategy for improving your memory abilities EXCEPT _____.
    a. Developing your motivation
    b. Practicing memory skills
    c. Staying focused and minimizing distractions
    d. Learning to rely on your memory alone

20. The letters in the SQ3R method stand for _____.
    a. San, question, rehearse, recite, retrieve
    b. Survey, question, read, recite, review
    c. Summarize, quantify, read, rehearse, review
    d. Survey, quantify, retrieve, rehearse, review

Answers and Explanations to Multiple Choice Posttest

1.

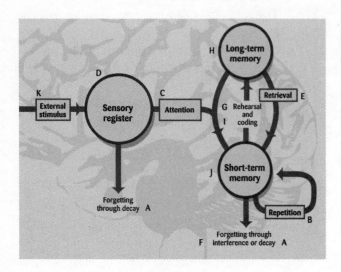

2. a. Visual sensations flow from your senses into the sensory registers. p. 202

3. b. What we are thinking of at any given moment refers to short-term memory. p. 205

4. b. Chunking is grouping information in meaningful units in short-term memory. p. 205

5. a. Elaborative rehearsal relates new information to something we already know. p. 209

6. c. Retrograde amnesia is the inability to recall events preceding an accident or injury, but without loss of earlier memory. p. 216

7. c. Semantic memory stores general facts and information. p. 211

8. b. Implicit memory provides retrieval cues we may not be aware of having made. p. 211

9. b. Old material interfering with remembering new material is called proactive interference. p. 217

10. d. Reconstructive memory changes the original memory. p. 219

11. d. Childhood amnesia refers to the difficulty adults have remembering experiences before age 2. p. 224

12. a. Autobiographical memory is collection of memories for events that took place in our lives. p. 223

13. b. Flashbulb memories are vivid memories of certain events and incidents surrounding them even long after the event occurred. p. 224–5

14. a. Similarity of material can lead to greater amounts of interference. p. 217

15. a. Mnemonic devices are techniques that make material easier to remember. p. 221

16. a. The hippocampus is important in converting short-term memory into long-term memory. p. 214

17. d. Acetylcholine is the neurotransmitter that is instrumental in memory. p. 217

18. c. Faulty eyewitness testimony was the single most persuasive element leading to false conviction in over 1,000 cases studied. p. 219

19. d. Rely on more than memory alone by using other tools. p. 221

20. b. Survey, question, read, recite, review is the correct order of the SQ3R method. p. 222

Information-processing model	Rote rehearsal
Sensory registers	Elaborative rehearsal
Attention	Retrograde anmesia
Short-term memory (STM)	Long-term memory (LTM)
Chunking	Semantic memory

Retaining information in short term memory simply by repeating it over and over.	A computerlike model used to describe the way humans encode, store, and retrieve information.
The linking of new information in short-term memory to familiar material stored in long-term memory.	Entry points for raw information from the senses.
Inability to recall events preceding an accident or injury, but without loss of earlier memory.	Selection of some incoming information for further processing.
Portion of memory that is more or less permanent corresponding to everything we "know."	Working memory; briefly stores and processes selected information from the sensory registers.
Portion of long-term memory that stores general facts and information.	Grouping of information into meaningful units for easier handling by short-term memory.

Episodic memory	Schema
Explicit memory	Flashbulb memory
Implicit memory	Mnemonics
Retroactive interference	Memory
Proactive interference	Serial position effect

Set of beliefs or expectation about something that is based on past experience.	Portion of long-term memory that stores personally experienced events.
A vivid memory of a certain event and the incidents surrounding it even after a long time has passed.	Memory for information that we can readily express in words and are aware of having, and can be intentionally retrieved from memory.
Techniques that make material easier to remember.	Memory for information that we cannot readily express in words and may not be aware of having, these memories cannot be intentionally retrieved from memory.
The ability to remember the things that we have experienced, imagined, and learned.	Process by which new information interferes with old information already in memory.
The finding that when asked to recall a list of unrelated items, performance is better for items at the beginning and end of the list.	Process by which information already in memory interferes with new information.

Procedural memory	
Emotional memory	
Childhood amnesia	

	The portion of long term memory that stores information relating, to skills, habits, and other preceptual-motor tasks.
	Learned emotional responses to various stimuli.
	The difficulty adults have remembering experiences from their first 2 years of life.

7

Cognition and Mental Abilities

C L A S S   A N D   T E X T   N O T E S

Use this section for class and text notes. Distinguish between lecture notes, textbook concepts, topics emphasized on the exams and your own comments.

Cognition

1. Building Blocks of Thought   page 231

    A. Language

        • Phonemes

        • Morphemes

        • Grammar

            – Syntax

            – Semantics

        • Surface structure

        • Deep structure

    B. Images

    C. Concepts

        • Prototypes

2. Language, Thought, and Culture   page 235

    A. Linguistic Relativity Hypothesis

---

3. Problem Solving   page 237

    A. The Interpretation of Problems

        • Problem representation

    B. Producing Strategies and Evaluation Progress

        • Trial and error

        • Information retrieval

        • Algorithms

        • Heuristics

            – Hill climbing

            – Subgoals

            – Means-end analysis

            – Working backwards

    C. Obstacles to Solving Problems

        • Set

        • Functional fixedness

        • Brainstorming

UNDERSTANDING Ourselves: Becoming a More Skillful Problem Solver   page 242

        • Eliminate poor choices

        • Visualize a solution

        • Develop expertise

- Think Flexibly

  - Divergent Thinking

  - Convergent Thinking

---

4. Decision Making   page 245

   A. Logical Decision Making

      - Compensatory

   B. Decision Making Heuristics

      - Representativeness heuristic

      - Availability

      - Confirmation bias

   C. Explaining Our Decisions

      - Framing

      - Hindsight

      - "If Only"

---

5. Intelligence and Mental Abilities   page 247

   Intelligence

   A. Theories of Intelligence

      - Early theorists

        - Spearman's general intelligence

        - Thurstone's 7 kinds of mental abilities

      - Spatial ability

      - Memory

- Perceptual speed

- Word fluency

- Numerical ability

- Reasoning

- Verbal meaning

  – Cattell's crystallized and fluid intelligence

- Crystallized intelligence

- Fluid intelligence

Contemporary Theorists

  –Sternberg's Triarchic Theory of Intelligence

- Componential intelligence

- Experiential intelligence

- Contextual intelligence

  – Gardner's Theory of Multiple Intelligences

- Logical-mathematical intelligence

- Linguistic intelligence

- Spatial intelligence

- Musical intelligence

- Bodily kinesthetic intelligence

- Interpersonal intelligence

- Intrapersonal Intelligence

- Naturalistic intelligence (recently added)

  – Goleman's Emotional Intelligence

- Knowing one's own emotions

- Managing one's emotions

- Using emotions to motivate oneself

- Recognizing the emotions of other people

- Managing relationships

B. Intelligence Tests

- The Stanford-Binet Intelligence Scale

  - Intelligence quotient (IQ)

- Wechsler Intelligence Scales

  - Wechsler Adult Intelligence Scale (WAIS-III)

  - Wechsler Intelligence Scale for Children (WISC-III)

- Group Tests

- Performance Tests and Culture-Fair Tests

  - Performance Tests

  - Culture-Fair Tests

C. What Makes a Good Test?

- Reliability

  - Split-half reliability

- Validity

  - Content validity

  - Criterion-related validity

- Criticisms of IQ Tests

- IQ and Success

3.

4.

5.

6.

7.

8.

9.

---

9.   Answers to Intelligence Test Questions   page 271

1.

2.

3.

4.

5.

6.

7.

8.

9.

Learning Objectives and Questions

After you have read and studied this chapter, you should be able to complete the following statements. Your exam is written based on these learning objectives.

LEARNING OBJECTIVES

1. Define cognition. Differentiate between images and concepts and explain the use of prototypes.

2. Explain Whorf's linguistic relativity hypothesis and summarize the evidence regarding links between language and thought.

3. Discuss proper interpretation and categorization in the problem solving process and how conceptual blocks may inhibit effective problem solving.

4. Compare and contrast divergent and convergent thinking and discuss their role in creative problem solving.

5. Identify three heuristics that may lead us to make poor decisions and explain how each one hinders effective decision-making.

6. Discuss Spearman's, Thurstone's and Cattell's models of intelligence and specifically describe the components of each model.

7. Describe Sternberg's and Gardner's theories of intelligence and how they differ from previous models of intelligence. List Sternberg's three types of intelligence and Gardner's seven multiple intelligences.

8. Name the people responsible for the development of intelligence tests for children. Include in your discussion key concepts such as IQ and how the formula for IQ was developed.

9. Distinguish between the Wechsler Adult Intelligence Scale-Revised (WAIS-R) and the Stanford Binet in terms of their focus. Identify the two parts of the WAIS-R.

10. Define performance tests and culture-fair tests. Discuss the necessity of such tests, where they are useful, and their advantages or disadvantages.

11. Define the terms reliability and validity and discuss two types of each.

12. Discuss the research findings on gender differences in mental abilities.

13. Define mental retardation. Identify the various levels of retardation and the necessary criteria for diagnosis. Discuss possible causes of retardation and effectiveness of treatment.

14. Discuss the criterion for giftedness. Summarize the research and criticisms of current techniques to measure giftedness. Discuss the advantages and possible disadvantages of accelerated classes for gifted students.

ESSAY QUESTIONS

1. Define language, phonemes, morphemes, semantics, syntax and grammar and briefly discuss the role of each of them in the development of communications and language.

2. Identify and describe four tactics for improving your problem-solving abilities and discuss the advantages of each method.

3. Compare and contrast compensatory and noncompensatory models and discuss the roles of representativeness, availability, and the confirmation bias in decision-making. Identify the strengths and weaknesses of each technique.

4. Explain "emotional intelligence". Identify the five traits of emotional intelligence.

5. Name at least 3 group IQ tests and 3 individual IQ tests. Explain the advantages and disadvantages of each. Include in your discussion their advantages and disadvantages.

6. Summarize current beliefs and research regarding the role of heredity and environment in intelligence. Include research on the effectiveness of intervention programs aimed at improving the academic performance of disadvantaged children.

7. Define creativity and discuss its relationship to intelligence. Identify four types of creativity tests and how they measure creativity.

Language Support

Students identified the following words from the text as needing more explanation. This page can be cut-out, folded in half, and used as a bookmark for this chapter.

A

Accelerate	cause to move faster, quicken the progress or development of
Accentuate	emphasize, make more prominent or intense, bring attention to
Acne	primarily an adolescent skin disorder marked by pimples on the face
AIDS	Acquired immune deficiency syndrome; life threatening disease
Ascent	rise upward, advance in status or reputation

B

Baffled	confused, puzzled, doubt or become perplexed
Brilliant	unusual mental keenness or alertness; very bright

C

Capitalize on	gain by turning something to advantage, profit from
Circumvent	get around something by using a strategy or cleverness
Civil service	government administrative job determined by competitive exam
Clarify	to make clear or understandable, free from confusion
Clear-cut	completely evident, definite, unambiguous, with clearly defined borders
Collaboration	working jointly with others, especially in an intellectual endeavor
Complacency	self satisfied state which may lack awareness of danger, unconcerned
Concede	to acknowledge hesitantly or grudgingly
Conceivably	possibly, perhaps, by chance
(In) Conjunction	being in association or union with; combined events or circumstances
Cross-reference	relate information from one source to another, check
Curiosity	desire to know, interest leading to inquiry

D

Deficit	lack or impairment in capacity to function
Detrimental	drawback, harmful or able to cause damage
Dispute	quarrel, debate, verbal argument that persists
Deteriorate	make worse, wear away, disintegrate
Dread	fear greatly or feel reluctant about something

E

Enmeshed	caught up or entangled in
Entity	independent, separate and distinct existence of a being
Equilateral	having all sides or faces equal
Excel	surpass in achievement or accomplishment, superior performance
Exhausted	extremely tired, used up or empty

F

Figurative	saying one thing normally indicating another regarded as being similar
Flawed	defect in structure or form, imperfection that hinders effectiveness
Fluency	effortless, smooth, rapid, expressed with ease
Foster	promote the growth or development of
Fuzzy	indistinct, lacking in clarity or definition

G

Grapple	struggle or wrestle, try to come to grips with
Guarantee	assert confidently, give security to

H

Hamper	to restrict with obstacles, hold back, restrain or impede
Hierarchy	ranked or graded series, classification or order
Hinder	slow or make difficult the progress of, hold back

I

Inherent	by nature or habit; essential characteristic of something
Innovation	introduce a new idea, method or device
Inquisitive	inclined to ask questions; curious; wanting to examine and learn
Interaction	mutual or reciprocal action or influence

J

Juggle	handle or deal with several things at once to satisfy competing requirements

K

Kinesthetic	having to do with body tension, movement and sensation
Knack	special ability that is difficult to teach or understand

L

Lanky	ungracefully tall and thin
Literally	reproduced word for word; exactly
Lobby	attempt to influence or sway towards a desired action

M

Maladjusted	lacking harmony with one's environment by poor or inadequate adjustment
Malnutrition	faulty or inadequate nutrition
Manifest	make evident by showing or displaying
Marshal	to bring together and order in an effective way
Merit	to be worthy of or entitled to; earn or deserve
Metaphorically	using a word or phase in place of another to suggest their similarity or likeness
Minimize	intentionally reduce or underestimate; play down
Modest	moderately estimating one's worth or ability; limited in size, amount or scope
Modify	limit or restrict, make less extreme, make basic changes in

N

Negligible	so small or unimportant or of such little consequence so as to warrant little or no attention
Notorious	widely known and discussed, usually unfavorably
Novice	beginner, un-experienced person

O

Obliterate	remove from memory or recognition; cause to disappear
Obscure	hide or conceal; cover or make indistinct; relatively unknown person
Offset	counterbalance or compensate for something else
Orphanage	an institution for the care of children without parents

P

Pantomime	convey a story by bodily or facial movements only
Paraprofessional	trained aide who assists a professional (i.e., a teacher, doctor or lawyer)
Pictorially	suggesting or conveying visual images
Prototype	standard or typical example; first functional form of a new design or construction

Q

Quantitative	express in terms of amount or measurement

R

Reiterate	state or do over again or repeat, sometimes with tiring effects
Remedial	concerned with correcting faulty study habits and raising a student's general competence; intended as a remedy
Resemblance	be like or similar to
Rule of thumb	general principle based on experience and common sense but not scientifically accurate

S

Shortcoming	lacking some necessary element, having a deficiency or inadequate
Shrewd	clever, perceptive, able to see what's hidden, practical
Signing hands	communicating by using sign language for the deaf
Sort out	examine for clarification, free from confusion, arrange by characteristics
Step-by-step	marked by successive, gradual degrees of limited progression
Stumped	frustrated, baffled, defeated by confusion
Stymied	stand in the way of; present an obstacle
Suspend	defer to a later time or specific condition
Sway	to fluctuate between positions or opinions; go back and forth

T

Tacit	without a stated contract or agreement, implied without verbal expression
Tactic	device, plan or method for accomplishing an end
Tangled	very involved or complex, giving the appearance of disorder

Y

Yearning	feeling tenderness or urgent longing; to desire or miss

Z

Zero in on	close in or focus attention on an objective

Multiple Choice Posttest

After studying the text and completing the Study Guide activities, answer these questions to determine if you need to review any areas before the course exam.

1. The three most important building blocks of thoughts are ____, _____, and ____.
   a. Semantics, phonemes, and morphemes
   b. Cognition, feelings, and language
   c. Language, images, and concepts
   d. Stream of consciousness, sensory register, and perception

2. Label the terms in correct order in the direction of movement in speech production and comprehension in the figure shown below.
   a. Phenomes
   b. Meaning
   c. Morphemes
   d. Sentences

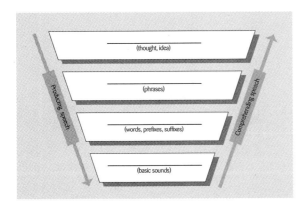

(thought, idea)

(phrases)

(words, prefixes, suffixes)

(basic sounds)

Producing speech

Comprehending speech

3. _____ consists of the language rules that determine how sounds and words can be combined and used to communicate meaning within a language.
   a. Semantics   c. Morphemes
   b. Syntax   d. Grammar

4. Most concepts that people use in thinking _____.
   a. Accurately account for critical differences among various images
   b. Depend on the magnitude of sensory memory
   c. Allow them to generalize but not to think abstractly
   d. Are fuzzy and overlap with one another

5. A mental model containing the most typical features of a concept is called a (n) ___.
   a. Algorithm
   b. Prototype
   c. Stereotype
   d. Description

6. The problem-solving methods that guarantee solutions if appropriate and properly followed are called _____.
   a. Heuristics
   b. Trial and error
   c. Hill-climbing
   d. Algorithm

7. The technique of ____ encourages people to generate a list of ideas without evaluation of those ideas.
   a. Convergent thinking
   b. Brainstorming
   c. Circular thinking
   d. Functional thinking

8. People sometimes make decisions based on information that is most easily retrieved from memory, even though this information may not be accurate. This process of decision-making is called _____.
   a. Compensatory model
   b. Means-end analysis
   c. The availability heuristic
   d. Functional analysis

9. The tendency to look for evidence in support of a belief and to ignore evidence that would disprove a belief is called _____.
   a. The confirmation bias
   b. Means-end analysis
   c. The representativeness heuristic
   d. Functional analysis

10. Spearman believed that specific mental abilities are ____ each other, and Thurstone believed that they are ___ each other.
    a. Dependent on; dependent on
    b. Dependent on; relatively independent of
    c. Relatively independent of; dependent on
    d. Relatively independent of; relatively independent of

11. According to Sternberg, the ability to capitalize on our strengths, compensate for our weaknesses and seek an environment n, which we can function most effectively, reflects ____ intelligence.
    a. Componential
    b. Exponential
    c. experiential
    d. contextual

12. Which of the following is NOT one of the types of intelligence described in Gardner's theory of multiple intelligences?
    a. practical intelligence
    b. interpersonal intelligence
    c. linguistic intelligence
    d. spatial intelligence

13. The Binet-Simon scale was originally developed to _____.
    a. Identify gifted children
    b. Identify children who might have difficulty in school
    c. Measure the intelligence of normal children
    d. Measure scholastic achievement

14. Wechsler hypothesized that adult intelligence _____.
    a. Consists of the ability to solve problems
    b. Consists solely of the ability to handle the environment
    c. Consists more of the ability to solve problems than of the ability to handle the environment
    d. Consists more of the ability to handle life situations than of skill in solving verbal and abstract problems.

15. Performance tests and culture-fair tests are similar in that they ____.
    a. Focus on linguistic abilities
    b. Are exclusively group tests
    c. Minimize or eliminate the use of words
    d. Focus only on mathematical and abstraction skills

16. The ability of a test to produce consistent and stable scores is its ____ while the ability of a test to measure what it sets out to measure is its _____.
    A. Validity; reliability
    B. Standard deviation; validity
    C. Reliability; validity
    D. Reliability; standard deviation

17. The largest program designed to improve educationally disadvantaged children's chances of school achievement is ____.
    a. The Milwaukee Project
    b. The Perry Preschool Program
    c. The Hobbs and Robinson Program
    d. The Head Start Program

18. Plomin's review of the literature on IQ led him to conclude that a person's IQ is about ___ percent the result of genetic factors and about ___ percent the result of environmental factors.
    a. 80; 20
    b. 70; 30
    c. 50; 50
    d. 30; 70

19. In the majority of cases the cause of both mental retardation and giftedness is ____.
    a. Clearly identified genetic abnormalities
    b. Unknown
    c. Poor prenatal nutrition
    d. Financial status of the parents

20. Creative people are ___ than less creative people with equivalent IQ scores.
    a. More intelligent in their actual job performance
    b. Perceived as being more intelligent
    c. Less intelligent in their actual job performance
    d. Perceived as being less intelligent

21. The type of thinking required to solve problems requiring a creative or flexible, or inventive solution is ____, and the type of thinking needed to solve problems requiring one or a few logically thought out solutions is _____.
    a. Functional thinking; circular thinking
    b. Convergent thinking; divergent thinking
    c. Divergent thinking; functional thinking
    d. Divergent thinking; convergent thinking

22. Each of the following is a characteristic of emotional intelligence EXCEPT:
    a. Knowing your emotions
    b. Using your emotions to motivate yourself
    c. Expressing your emotions
    d. Managing relationships

Answers and Explanations to Multiple Choice Posttest

1. c. Thoughts are believed to be made up of language, images and concepts. pp. 231–2

2. Top to bottom: b. meaning; d. sentences; c. morphemes; a. phenomes Fig. 7–1; p. 233

3. d. The language rules that determine how to combine and use sounds and words to communicate are called grammar. p. 232

4. d. Most people use fuzzy, poorly defined and overlapping concept. p. 234

5. b. A prototype is a mental model containing representative features of a concept. p. 234

6. d. Algorithms are step-by-step problem solving methods that guarantee a correct solution. p. 239

7. b. Brainstorming involves generating numerous ideas before evaluating them. p. 243

8. c. The availability heuristic relies on the information most easily retrieved from long-term memory. p. 245

9. a. Confirmation bias causes us to find evidence to support our beliefs. p. 245

10. b. Spearman believed that intelligence is generalized to specific mental abilities; while Thurstone believed they are relatively independent of each other. p. 248

11. d. Contextual intelligence capitalizes on strengths, compensates for weaknesses and seeks an effective environment in which to function. p. 249

12. a. Practical intelligence is not a type of multiple intelligence. p 250

13. b. The Binet-Simon scale was developed in 1905 to identify children that might have difficulty in school. p. 251

14. d. Wechsler believed that adult intelligence is more concerned with the ability to handle life situations than excel at verbal or mathematical problems. p. 252

15. c. Both performance tests and culture fair tests were designed to eliminate or minimize words and language. p. 253

16. c. Reliability measures a test's ability to produce stable, consistent scores; and validity effectively measures what a test has been designed to measure. p. 254

17. d. The Head Start Program is the largest program created to enrich disadvantaged children's educational opportunities. p. 260

18. c. Plomin found that heredity and environment almost equally contributed to human differences in intelligence. p. 261

19. b. As with mental retardation, the causes of giftedness are largely unknown. p. 265

20. b. Creative people are perceived as being more intelligent than their less creative but equivalent IQ score counterparts. p. 266

21. d. Divergent thinking reflects original, inventive and flexible thinking; convergent thinking is directed towards finding one correct solution. p. 242

22. c. Expressing your emotions is NOT one of the 5 traits of emotional intelligence. p. 250

Key Vocabulary Terms

Cut out each term and use as study cards.
Definition is on the back side of each term.

Cognition	Concept
Phonemes	Prototype
Morphemes	Linguistic relativity hypothesis
Grammar	Problem representation
Image	Algorithm

A mental category for classifying objects, people, or experiences.

The process whereby we acquire and use knowledge.

According to Rosch, a mental model containing the most typical feature of a concept.

The basic sounds that make up any language.

Whorf's idea that patterns of thinking are determined by the specific language one speaks.

The smallest meaningful units of speech, such as simple words, prefixes, and suffixes.

The first step in solving a problem; it involves interpreting or defining the problem.

The language rules that determine how sounds and words can be combined and used to communicate meaning within a language.

A step-by-step method of problem solving that guarantees a correct solution.

A mental representation of a sensory experience.

Heuristics	Mental Set
Hill climbing	Functional fixedness
Subgoals	Divergent thinking
Means-end analysis	Convergent thinking
Working backward	Brainstorming

Tendency to perceive and to approach problems in certain ways.

Rules of thumb that help in simplifying and solving problems, although they do not guarantee a correct solution.

The tendency to perceive only a limited number of uses for an object, thus interfering with the process of problem solving.

A heuristic problem solving strategy in which each step moves you progressively closer to the final goal.

Thinking that meets the criteria of originality, inventiveness, and flexibility.

Intermediate, more manageable goals used in one heuristic strategy to make it easier to reach the final goal.

Thinking that is directed toward one correct solution to a problem.

A heuristic strategy that aims to reduce the discrepancy between the current situation and the desired goal at a number of intermediate points.

A problem-solving strategy in which an individual or a group produces numerous ideas and evaluates them only after all ideas are collected.

A heuristic strategy in which one works backward from the desired goal to the given conditions.

Compensatory model	Componential intelligence
Representativeness heuristic	Experiential intelligence
Availability heuristic	Contextual intelligence
Confirmation bias	Intelligence quotient (IQ)
Intelligence	Wechsler Adult Intelligence Scale

According to Sternberg, the ability to acquire new knowledge, to solve problems effectively.

A rational decision-making model in which choices are systematically evaluated on various criteria.

Accordingly to Sternberg, the ability to adapt creatively in new situations, to use insight.

A heuristic by which a new situation is judged on the basis of its resemblance to a stereo-typical model.

According to Sternberg, the ability to select contexts in which you can excel, to shape the environment to fit your strengths.

A heuristic by which a judgment or decision is based on information that is most easily retrieved from memory.

A numerical value given to intelligence that is determined from the scores on an intelligence test; based on a score of 100 for average intelligence.

The tendency to look for evidence in support of a belief and to ignore evidence that would disprove a belief.

An individual intelligence test developed especially for adults; measures both verbal and performance abilities.

A general term referring to the ability or abilities involved in learning and adaptive behavior.

Wechsler Scale for Children	Split-half reliability
Group test	Validity
Performance tests	Content validity
Culture-fair tests	Criterion-related validity
Reliability	Mental retardation

A method of determining test reliability by dividing the test into two parts and checking the agreement of scores on both parts.

An individual intelligence test developed especially for school-aged children; measures verbal and performance abilities and also yields an overall IQ score.

Ability of a test to measure what it has been designed to measure.

Written intelligence tests administered by one examiner to many people at one time.

Refers to a test's having an adequate sample of the skills or knowledge it is supposed to measure.

Intelligence tests that minimize the use of language.

Validity of a test as measured by a comparison of the test score and independent measures of what the test is designed to measure.

Intelligence tests designed to eliminate cultural bias by minimizing skills and values that vary from one culture to another.

Condition of significantly subaverage intelligence combined with deficiencies in adaptive behavior.

Ability of a test to produce consistent and stable scores.

Giftedness	Counterfactual thinking
Creativity	Intelligence
Language	Triarchic theory of intelligence
Framing	Theory of multiple intelligences
Hindsight	Emotional intelligence

Thinking about alternative realities and things that never happened (i.e., "what if"?)	Refers to superior IQ combined with demonstrated or potential ability in such areas as academic aptitude, creativity, or leadership.
A general term referring to the ability or abilities involved in learning and adaptive behavior.	The ability to produce novel and socially valued ideas or objects.
Sternberg's theory that intelligence involves mental skills (componential), insight and creative adaptability (experiential) and environmential responsiveness (contextual.)	A flexible system of communication that uses sounds, rules, gestures, on symbols to convey information.
Gardner's theory that there are many intelligences, each one relatively independent of the others. He lists 7 types of multiple intelligence.	The perspective from which we interpret information before making a decision.
Goleman's theory that one form of intelligence refers to how effectively people perceive and understand their own emotions and the emotions of others, and can regulate and manage their emotional behavior.	Thinking about alternative realities and things that never happened.

8

Motivation and Emotion

C L A S S   A N D   T E X T   N O T E S

Use this section for class and text notes. Distinguish between lecture notes, textbook concepts, topics emphasized on the exams and your own comments.

Motive

Emotion

1. Perspectives on Motivation   page 278

    A. Instincts

    B. Drive-Reduction Theory

        • Homeostasis

        • Primary Drives

        • Secondary Drives

    C. Arousal Theory

        • Yerkes-Dodson Law

        • Incentives

    D. Intrinsic and Extrinsic Motivation

    E. A Hierarchy of Motives

        • Maslow's Hierarchical Model

            – Physiological needs

– Safety needs

– Belongingness needs

– Esteem needs

– Self-actualization needs

---

2. Hunger and Thirst p. 282

   A. Biological and Emotional Factors

   B. Cultural and Social Factors

   C. Eating Disorders

- Anorexia nervosa

- Bulimia

   D. Weight Control

UNDERSTANDING Ourselves   page 286

The Slow (but Lasting) Fix for Weight Gain

   1. Check with your doctor first

   2. Increase your metabolism through regular exercise

   3. Modify your diet

   4. Reduce external cues encouraging you to eat

   5. Reward yourself for small improvements

---

3. Sex   page 287

   A. Biological factors

- Testosterone

- Pheromones

- Sexual Response Cycle

  – Excitement

  – Plateau

  – Orgasm

  – Resolution

B. Cultural and Environmental Factors

C. Sexual Orientation

  - Heterosexual

  - Homosexual

  - Bisexual

---

4. Other Important Motives   page 291

Stimulus Motives

A. Exploration and Curiosity

B. Manipulation and Contact

C. Aggression

  - Biological or Learned?

  - Aggression and Culture

  - Gender and Aggression

D. Achievement

  - Achievement motive

  - Thematic Apperception Test (TAT)

D. Affiliation

  - Affiliation motive

What Motivates Rape?

5.   Emotions   page 299

    A. Basic Emotions

    B. Theories of Emotion

       • James Lange Theory

       • Cannon-Bard Theory

       • Cognitive Theories of Emotions

       • Challenges

---

6.   Communicating Emotion   page 303

    A. Voice Quality and Facial Expression

    B. Body Language, Personal Space, and Gestures

       • Explicit acts

    C. Gender and Emotion

    D. Culture and Emotion

       • Universalist position

       • Cultural learning

       • Display rules

Learning Objectives and Questions

After you have read and studied this chapter, you should be able to complete the following statements. Your exam is written based on these learning objectives

LEARNING OBJECTIVES

1. Define motive and emotion and explain the roles of stimulus, behavior, and goals in motivation.

2. Explain the functioning of the primary drive of hunger. Discuss those mechanisms in the brain that regulate this drive and which external and cultural factors affect perceptions of hunger.

3. Define anorexia nervosa and bulimia, discuss their prevalence, symptoms, who is most likely to develop them, and current treatment.

4. Compare and contrast the sex drive with other primary drives. Describe the biological and psychological factors involved in sexual arousal. Summarize current beliefs about differences in sexual orientation.

5. Summarize the research on aggression in humans in terms of the causes of aggression, methods for modifying aggressive behavior, and cultural and gender differences in aggression.

6. Distinguish between the motives for achievement, affiliation, and power. Explain why these needs are so strong in some people.

7. List and define the five levels of Maslow's hierarchy of motives. Describe how these needs affect people's everyday lives and goals.

8. Compare and contrast the James-Lange, Cannon-Bard, and cognitive theories of emotion.

9. Explain and name the eight parts of the scheme for categorizing emotion created by Plutchik.

10. Discuss gender differences in the experience and expression of emotion. Be certain to dispel any myths about male and female emotional responsiveness.

11. Discuss the similarities and differences in facial expression of emotions across cultures. Name those facial expressions considered to be 'universal' in emotional meaning.

ESSAY QUESTIONS

1. Discuss Harlow's experiments with infant monkeys and 'surrogate mothers'. Discuss the need for contact and whether or not it is universal and applies to other organisms besides humans. How do Harlow's findings generalize to human infant development of attachment?

2. Discuss the most effective methods for losing weight and maintaining the weight loss. Provide the 5 Steps for Losing Weight outlined in the text.

3. Compare and contrast verbal and nonverbal communication in expressing emotion. Give at least three examples of nonverbal communication and how each assists in sending an emotional message. Explain why some people may not be willing or able to report their emotions verbally.

4. Identify and discuss the different types of sexual coercion. Describe what factors contribute to sexual coercion (i.e., motivation of the perpetrator) and the impact it has on the victims.

5. Discuss the characteristics of the stimulus motives of activity, exploration, curiosity, manipulation and contact. Provide an example of each and discuss how they may contribute to changes in behavior and society.

Language Support

Students identified the following words from the text as needing more explanation. This page can be cut-out, folded in half, and used as a bookmark for this chapter.

A

Accomplice	one associated with another especially in wrongdoing
Acutely	sudden onset, sharp rise, severe
Adjacent	immediately preceding or following, in close proximity, adjoining
Agile	able to move with grace and ease; quick resourceful, adaptable character
Agitation	to excite or trouble the mind or feelings; attempt to arouse public emotion
Amalgamation	put two or more things together; merge; unite; link or adhere
Aphrodisiac	food or drug that arouses sexual desire; something that excites

B

Beeline	to go quickly in a straight direct course
Bristle	assume an aggressive attitude or appearance when slighted
Bungee jumping	jumping off a high structure attached to a cord so the body springs back before hitting the ground or water

C

Charitable donation	liberal in giving to the needy, generosity in contributing to causes
Cinematic violence	violence portrayed in the movies
Contact sports	any sport that allows physical contact between the players
Consecutive	following one after the other in order
Continuum	progressive sequence or series with no discernable division
Counterproductive	tending to hinder the attainment of a desired goal
Courtesy	considerate, cooperative and polite
Conversely	in reversed order, relation or action
Crime ring	gang or group involved in criminal activity

D

Decoding	convert into understandable form; discover underlying meaning
Degrade	lower in rank or status; demote; drop to less effective level; low esteem
Deviate	to depart from norms of society; stray from standard principle or topic
Differentiate	perceive or show a marked difference from other things; distinguish
Discourage	to dissuade or talk out of; hold back by not encouraging, lose confidence
Drastic	extreme or severe action or effect
Drumming fingers	tapping one's fingers rhythmically on a hard surface

E

Emaciated	wasting away physically; very thin or feeble
Embrace	take up readily; welcome or avail oneself of something
Encompass	enclose; envelop; include; form a circle around
Exotic	striking, exciting, or mysteriously different or unusual

F

Fervor	intensity of feeling or expression
Fluctuations	continual change; shift back and forth; irregular movements
Fretting	feel or express worry, annoyance, emotional strain

G

Goosebumps	bristling of hair on skin from cold, fear or sudden excitement
Gory	unpleasant or sensational; bloody
Graphic	depicted in a realistic or vivid manner, i.e., graphic sex or violence

Gravitate	to be strongly attracted or drawn to; move under gravitational force
Growl	deep guttural sound of anger or hostility; murmur or complain, grumble
H	
Hold in check	to stop the movement, rate or intensity of; restrain
Hypothetical	an inference from unproven evidence; conclusion deduced by guessing
I	
Impostor	one that assumes false identity for the purpose of deception
Inaccurate	incorrect or untrue
Inconclusive	leading to no clear result
Infallible	unfailing in effectiveness; absolutely trustworthy
Inflict	cause someone to endure something unpleasant
Inordinate	exceeding reasonable limits; excessive
Insignificant	lacking influence; small in stature or quantity
Instantaneous	occurring without delay; presently
Interplay	reciprocal relationship, action or influence from one to another
In the midst of	in the middle of an action or situation; surrounded by or in proximity to others
In the closet	secretly homosexual while appearing heterosexual
Irritability	quick to anger, become annoyed or impatient
L	
Limp	lacking firm substance, strength or vigor; spiritless
Lush	plush; fertile; prosperous; plentiful
M	
Mundane	commonplace, ordinary, practical
N	
Night owl	person who keeps late night hours
Nostalgia	sentimental yearning for return to the past or something lost
O	
Optimum	most favorable condition for growth; greatest degree attainable
Orientation	general direction or tendency of one's thoughts, inclinations or acts
Overestimate	overrate, hold in too high esteem or value
P	
Pep talk	brief, intense, emotional talk designed to encourage an audience
Pornographic	depicting erotic behavior in art, film or writing intended to cause sexual excitement
Portrayed	describe in words or picture; enact; play role of; reveal; expose
Premium	exceptional quality or amount; in demand
Presume	take for granted; act without clarity; believe to be true without proof
Predisposition	inclined to; leaning or drawn toward a belief or type of conduct
Prevalent	generally widely accepted, favored or practiced; widespread
Propensity	an intense, natural inclination or preference towards
Provocation	arouse, incite, stimulate, anger or annoy
Puny	slight or inferior in power, size or importance
R	
Rampant	without restraint; widespread; unchecked
Recrimination	accusation in return; countercharging an accuser
Replenish	fill or rebuild; inspire, make good or powerful again
Revenge	opportunity to get even or satisfaction; retaliate in kind
S	
Solicit	approach with request or plea; urge strongly or ask others for
Spectacular	sensational; exceedingly elaborate or grand
Strive	devote serious effort or energy; endeavor; attempt

Strychnine	poisonous plant used in medicine to stimulate the central nervous system
Succumb	yield to superior strength or force; overpowering desire; death
Surrogate	one that serves as a substitute
T	
Taunt	tease; provoke; challenge or insult; use of sarcasm
Tendency	inclination or purposeful movement in a particular direction
Trample	crush or step on heavily; be harshly domineering over
Turbulent	causing disturbance, agitation, unrest
Turn one's stomach	to disgust completely; sicken; nauseate
U	
Unmanly	of weak character; cowardly; effeminate
V	
Vestige	traces; marks or visible signs left by something
Vigorous	strong, energetic, forceful mental or physical strength, active force
W	
Wafting	to move lightly as if by the impulse of wind or waves
Wreak havoc	bring about or cause destruction

Multiple Choice Posttest

After studying the text and completing the Study Guide activities, answer these questions to determine if you need to review any areas before the course exam.

1. A (n) _____ is a need that pushes a person to work toward a specific goal.
   a. Stimulus
   b. Behavior
   c. Incentive
   d. Motive

2. A (n) _____ is an inborn, goal-directed behavior that is seen in an entire species.
   a. Instinct
   b. Drive
   c. Motive
   d. Stimulus

3. External stimuli that lead to goal-directed behavior are called _____.
   a. Drives
   b. Incentives
   c. Needs
   d. Reciprocals

4. All of the following are examples of primary drives EXCEPT
   a. Hunger
   b. Money
   c. Thirst
   d. Affiliation

5. A desire to perform a behavior that originates within the individual is known as _____, while a desire to perform a behavior to obtain an external reward or avoid punishment is known as _____.
   a. Primary motivation; secondary motivation
   b. Intrinsic motivation; extrinsic motivation
   c. Secondary motivation; primary motivation
   d. Extrinsic motivation; intrinsic motivation

6. Increased _____ is the most effective way to increase the body's metabolism when trying to lose weight.
   a. Protein consumption
   b. Exercise
   c. Reduction of calories
   d. Sleep

7. A serious eating disorder that is associated with an intense fear of weight gain and a distorted body image is called _____.
   a. Anorexia nervosa
   b. Karposi's anemia
   c. bulimia
   d. Huntington's chorea

8. An eating disorder characterized by binges of eating followed by self-induced vomiting or purging is called _____.
   a. Anorexia nervosa
   b. Karposi's anemia
   c. bulimia
   d. Huntington's chorea

9. In Harlow's classic experiments, when the infant monkeys were frightened, they ran to a "surrogate mother" that offered _____.
   a. food and warmth
   b. food only
   c. warmth only
   d. warmth and closeness

10. Scents that can be sexually stimulating are called _____.
    a. androgens
    b. corticorsteroids
    c. globulins
    d. pheromones

11. The correct chronological order of the phases of the sexual response cycle is _____.
    a. resolution, excitement, plateau, orgasm
    b. excitement, resolution, orgasm, plateau
    c. plateau, excitement, orgasm, resolution
    d. excitement, plateau, orgasm, resolution

12. _____ are largely unlearned motives that push us to investigate, explore, and often change, the world around us.
    a. Primary drives
    b. Stimulus drives
    c. Secondary motives
    d. Achievement drives

13. Research indicates that _____ factors contribute to gender differences in aggressive behavior.
    a. neither biological nor social
    b. biological, but not social
    c. social, but not biological
    d. both social and biological

14. Which one of the following is NOT of the three separate, but interrelated aspects of achievement-oriented behavior identified by Helmrich and Spence?
   a. work-orientation   c. mastery
   b. curiosity   d. competitiveness

15. Label the correct sequential order of Maslow's hierarchy of motives from the most primitive to the most complex and human, using the following needs:
   a. belongingness   c. safety
   b. esteem   d. self-
   e. physiological   actualization

16. The _____ theory of emotion states that the experience of emotion occurs simultaneously with biological changes.
   a. Cannon-Bard   c. Schacter-Singer
   b. James-Lange   d. cognitive

17. The belief that certain facial expressions represent similar emotions across all cultures is known as the _____ position.
   a. universalist   c. culture-learning
   b. fundamentalist   d. unidimensional

18. Recent research indicates that sexual motivation is the predominant motive in rapes about ___ percent of the time.
   a. 30   c. 70
   b. 50   d. 90

Answers and Explanations to Multiple Choice Posttest

1. d. Motives are needs that push people to work toward specific goals. pp. 277–278

2. a. Instincts are inborn, goal-directed behavior seen in an entire species. p. 278

3. c. Incentives are external stimuli that lead to goal-directed behavior. p. 279

4. c. Primary needs are basic needs we are born with, such as hunger, thirst, sexual drive and comfort. p. 278

5. b. Intrinsic motivation originates with the individual, and extrinsic motivation originates from the desire to obtain an external reward. pp. 279–280

6. c. Exercise is the best way to prevent metabolism from dropping when dieting. p. 286

7. a. Anorexia nervosa is a serious eating disorder associated with intense fear of weight gain and a distorted body image. p. 284

8. c. Bulimia is an eating disorder characterized by eating and purging binges. p. 285

9. d. The surrogate mothers chosen by the infant monkeys offered warmth and closeness. p. 292

10. d. Pheromones are sexually stimulating scents produced by the body. p. 288

11. d. The correct chronological order of the sexual response cycle is: excitement, plateau, orgasm and resolution. p. 288

12. b. Stimulus drives are unlearned motives that push us to investigate and explore. p. 291

13. d. Both sociological and biological factors contribute to gender differences in aggressive behavior. p. 296

14. b. Curiosity is NOT one of the achievement-oriented behavioral aspects. p. 297

15. Maslow's hierarchy of motives from primitive to complex is: e. physiological; c. safety; a. belongingness; b. esteem and d. self-actualization. p. 281, Fig. 8–2

16. b.   The James-Lange theory of emotions states emotion and biological changes occur simultaneously. p. 300

17. a.   The universalist position holds that certain facial expressions represent similar emotions across all cultures. p. 306; Fig. 8-6 on p. 301

18. b.   Sexual motivation is the predominant motive in 50% of rapes. p. 295

Key Vocabulary Terms

Cut out each term and use as study cards.
Definition is on the back side of each term.

Motive	Homeostasis
Emotion	Incentive
Instinct	Intrinsic motivation
Drive	Extrinsic motivation
Drive-reduction theory	Primary drive

State of balance and stability in which the organism functions effectively.

Specific need or desire, such as hunger, thirst, or achievement, that prompts goal-oriented behavior.

External stimulus that prompts goal-directed behavior.

Feeling, such as fear, joy, surprise and anger that energizes and directs behavior.

A desire to perform a behavior that originates within the individual or the activity itself.

Inborn, inflexible, goal-directed behavior that is characteristic of an entire species.

A desire to perform a behavior to obtain an external reward or avoid punishment.

State of tension or arousal due to biological needs.

An unlearned drive, such as hunger, that is based on a physiological state.

States that motivated behavior is aimed at reducing a state of bodily tension or arousal and returning the organism to homeostasis.

Anorexia nervosa	Yerkes-Dodson law
Bulimia	James-Lange theory
Stimulus motive	Cannon-Bard theory
Achievement motive	Cognitive theory
Affiliation motive	Display rules

States there is optimal level of arousal for the best performance of any task; the more complex the task, the lower the level of arousal that can be tolerated before performance deterioration.

A serious eating disorder that is associated with an intense fear of weight gain and a distorted body image.

States that stimuli cause physiological changes in our bodies, and emotions result from those physiological changes.

An eating disorder characterized by binges of eating followed by self-induced vomiting.

States that the experience of emotion occurs simultaneously with biological changes.

Unlearned motive, such as curiosity or contact, that prompts us to explore or change the world around us.

States that emotional experiences depend on one's perception or judgment of the situation one is in.

The need to excel, to overcome obstacles.

Culture-specific rules that govern how, when, and why expressions of emotion are displayed.

The need to be with others.

Secondary
drive

Arousal
theory

Aggression

A learned drive, such as ambition, that is not based on a physiological state.

Theory of motivation that propose that organisms seek an optimal level of arousal.

Behavior aimed at doing harm to others; also, the motive to behave aggressively.

Life Span Development

C L A S S   A N D   T E X T   N O T E S

Use this section for class and text notes. Distinguish between lecture notes, textbook concepts, topics emphasized on the exams and your own comments.

1. Enduring Issues and Methods in Developmental Psychology   page 313

   A. Three Enduring Issues

      1. Individual Characteristics vs. Shared Human Traits

      2. Stability vs. Change

      3. Heredity vs. Environment

   B. Cross-sectional study

   C. Cohort

   D. Longitudinal studies

   E. Biographical study

2. Prenatal Development   page 315

   A. Embryo

   B. Fetus

   C. Placenta

   D. Critical period

3.   The Newborn Baby   page 317

A. Neonates

B. Reflexes

- Rooting

- Sucking

- Swallowing

- Grasping

- Stepping

C. Temperament

D. Perceptual Abilities

- Vision

- Depth perception

    – Visual cliff

- Other senses

---

4.   Infancy and Childhood   page 320

A. Physical Development

B. Motor Development

- Maturation

C. Cognitive Development

- Piaget's Stages of Cognitive Development

    1. Sensory-Motor Stage (Birth–2 yrs.)

    – Object permanence

    – Mental representation

2. Preoperational Stage (2–7 yrs.)

– Egocentric

3. Concrete Operational Stage (7–11 yrs.)

– Principles of conservation

Formal Operational Stage (11–15 yrs.)

- Criticisms of Piaget's Theory

D. Moral Development

- Kohlberg's Stages of Moral Reasoning

1. Preconventional Level

2. Conventional Level

3. Postconventional Level

E. Language Development

- Babbling

- Holophrases

- Theories of Language Development

- Skinner's Reinforcemento Reward

- Chomsky's Language Acquisition Device

– Language instinct

- Bilingualism and Success in School

F. Social Development

- Parent-Child Relationships in Infancy: Development of Attachment

– Imprinting

– Attachment

– Autonomy

– Socialization

- Parent-Child Relationships in Childhood

    – Erikson: Initiative vs. guilt

    – Parenting Styles

- Authoritarian

- Permissive

- Authoritative

- Relationships with Other Children

    – Solitary play

    – Parallel play

    – Cooperative play

    – Peer Group

- Erikson's Industry versus Inferiority

- Sex-Role Developmento Gender Identity

    – Gender Constancy

    – Gender-role Awareness

    – Gender Stereotypes

    – Sex-typed Behavior

G. Television and Children

---

5. Adolescence   page 337

A. Physical Changes

- Growth Spurt

- Sexual Development

    – Puberty

    – Menarche

UNDERSTANDING the World Around Us   page 344–345

Kids Who Kill

UNDERSTANDING Ourselves   page 348–349

Resolving Conflicts in Intimate Relationships

    B. The World of Work

- Dual-Career Families

- Children in Dual-Career Families

    C. Cognitive Changes

    D. Personality Changes

    E. Erikson's Generativity versus Stagnation

- Midlife Crisis and Transition

- Midlife Transition

    F. The "Change of Life"

- Menopause

---

7.   Late Adulthood   page 354

    A. Physical Changes

    B. Social Development

- Retirement

- Sexual Behavior

    C. Cognitive Changes

- Alzheimer's Disease

    D. Facing the End of Life

- Stages of Dying

  - Kubler-Ross's Five Stages

- Denial

- Anger

- Bargaining

- Depression

- Acceptance

  - Death Affirming Cultures

  - Death Denying Cultures

  - Widowhood

Learning Objectives and Questions

After you have read and studied this chapter, you should be able to complete the following statements. Your exam is written based on these learning objectives.

OBJECTIVES

1. Define developmental psychology and discuss some limitations of the methods used to study development.

2. Describe prenatal, infancy, and child development.

3. What are the four stages of Piaget's theory of cognitive development?

4. Trace language development from infancy through age 5 or 6.

5. Explain the importance of secure attachments between a caregiver and child.

6. Explain how sex-role identity is formed.

7. Summarize the important physical and cognitive changes that the adolescent undergoes during puberty.

8. Discuss the four problems of adolescence: self-esteem, depression, suicide, and eating disorders.

9. Distinguish between the longitudinal and cross-sectional methods as they relate to the study of adulthood. List the disadvantages of the methods and how the disadvantages can be overcome.

10. Identify the central concerns and crises that characterize the young, middle, and late adulthood stages. Explain moral development.

11. Identify Elisabeth Kübler-Ross' five sequential stages through which people pass as they react to their own impending death.

Language Support

Students identified the following words from the text as needing more explanation. This page can be cut-out, folded in half, and used as a bookmark for this chapter.

A

Abrupt	action or change without preparation or warning; stop or cut off
Accustomed	adapted to existing conditions; being in the habit of something
Acquisition	new, added or acquired characteristic, trait or ability; to get as one's own
Approach	to make advances in order to create a desired result in a particular manner
Awkward	lacking dexterity or skill, expertness or lacking ease and grace
Animosity	ill will or resentment leading to active hostility
Atrophy	decrease in size, arrested development or wasting away; degeneration

B

Bilingual	expressed in two languages, especially with equal fluency
Broadside	attack attack that is directed or placed sideways
Barrage	vigorous or rapid outpouring; projection of many things at once

C

Colicky	acute abdominal pain usually suffered by babies
Coincide	to be in agreement; correspond in nature, character or function
Cohabitation	to live in together as or as if a married couple
Callous	hardened; feeling noemotion or sympathy for others
Candid	honest, sincere without deception; may be frank, blunt or critical
Chaos	state of utter confusion; unpredictable behavior
Congenital	existing at birth; acquired during development in the uterus; not heredity

D

Depersonalization	deprive of the sense of personal identity; make impersonal
Devastate	reduce to chaos, disorder helplessness; bring to ruin by violent action
Discern	discriminate; see or understand the subtle differences
Dutiful	filled with or motivated by a sense of duty
Disparity	different, distinct in quality or character; inharmonious, incompatible elements
Distracted	mentally confused, troubled; may seem distant or aloof
Doleful look	expressing grief or sadness
Defuse	to make less harmful or tense
Dredge up	bring to light by deeply searching
Disengage	release or detach oneself form something that involves or engages; withdraw

E

Entrust	trust or put confidence in another person
Evidence	something that provides proof; an indication or outward sign

G

Grievance	complaint; cause of distress or a reason to complain or resist
Give and Take	making mutual concessions; compromise; usually good natured exchange of ideas or comments

H

Hazard	source of danger or risk
Hair trigger	immediate responsiveness to the slightest stimulus
Hard driving	

I

Implement	carry out, accomplish, means of expression; put in action
Incredible	to improbable or extraordinary to be believed
Inclusive	covering all items; broad in scope or orientation
Inevitable	unavoidable; cannot be evaded
Illustrate	make clear by giving an example; clarify
Indignity	insult, humiliate; treatment that undermines a person's dignity or self respect

L

Lament	wail; mourn aloud; strong expression of sorrow or regret

M

Milestones	significant points in development
Modify	make basic changes in or to
Mingle	associate; come in contact with; mix together without losing identity
Mislead	to deliberately lead astray in a wrong direction or action
Methodology	a discipline's body of rules and procedures

O

Odorous	strong distinctive smell whether pleasant or unpleasant
Outrage	arouse anger or resentment usually by a serious offense

P

Postpone	put off until a later time; delay
Palatial house	magnificent; similar to a palace; lavish and stately
Placid	serenely free of interruption or disturbance; calm
Pervade	to diffuse throughout every part; distribute, spread or scatter
Perpetually	valid for all time; lasting and enduring indefinitely

R

Rear	to bring a person to maturity through nurturing care and education
Reserved	restrained in words and actions
Revere	show devotion and honor to
Rudimentary	fundamental or basic principles
Rationale	underlying reasoning or explanation of opinion, belief or practice

S

Sacrifice	to give up or suffer a loss for an ideal, belief or desired end
Siblings	one of 2 or more children having common parents or things related by a common tie or characteristic
Shower	give in abundance; generosity
"Storm and stress"	(sturm und drang) high emotionalism and rousing action; turmoil
Superordinate	superior in rank, class or status
Span	exend across an individual's lifetime; a limited time period
Shrug off	play down; soft-pedal; minimize; brush aside; underestimate intentionally
Silent treatment	completely ignoring a person by silence as a means of expressing contempt or disapproval
Stagnant	not advancing or developing; not moving forward

T

Turmoil	extreme confusion, agitation or commotion
Tentative	doubt, indecision, uncertainty; hesitant to make a decision
Take stock of	take an inventory of resources or prospects
Taboo	banned, forbidden, not allowed, prohibited

U

Unpopular	viewed or received unfavorably by the public
Uninhibited	expressive, high spirited; boisterously informal

Usher in	mark or observe the beginning of; to bring into being
Unisex	not distinguishable as male or female; suitable or designed for both sexes
Ultimatum	final demand or condition whose rejection will lead another action
Undeniable	unquestionable true; genuine

V

| Vanish | pass quickly from sight or completely from existence; disappear |
| Victimize | subject to deception or fraud; cheat; make a victim of by objecting someone to hardship, oppression or mistreatment |

W

Wail	loud lament; prolonged cry of sound expressing grief, pain our mourning
Worthwhile	regarded as being worthy of the time or effort spent
Wronged	being injured unjustly

Z

| Zest | gusto, keen enjoyment, exciting quality |

Multiple Choice Posttest

After studying the text and completing the Study Guide activities, answer these questions to determine if you need to review any areas before the course exam.

1. Times when certain internal and external influences have a major impact on development, whereas at other times those same influences would have little impact, are called _____.
   a. Developmental surges
   b. Growth stages
   c. critical periods
   d. latency period

2. The term used by psychologists to describe the physical/emotional characteristics of the newborn child and young infant is _____.
   a. Cognitive capacity
   b. Temperament
   c. maturity
   d. development

3. People born during the same period of historical time are called ____.
   a. A cohort
   b. A cross-sectional group
   c. clique
   d. a peerage

4. Children have developed a capacity for self-recognition by the end of the ___ stage.
   a. Concrete operations
   b. Preoperational operations
   c. sensory motor
   d. formal

5. A characteristic that first shows up in the formal operations stage is ___.
   a. Irreversibility
   b. Abstract thinking
   c. egocentrism
   d. logical thinking

6. The _____ process teaches children what behaviors and attitudes are appropriate in their family, friendships and culture.
   a. attachment
   b. socialization
   c. imprinting
   d. anthropomorphism

7. Authoritative parents are to ____ children as permissive parents are to ____ children.
   a. Distrustful; assertive
   b. Self-reliant; dependent
   c. Passive; assertive
   d. Distrustful; dependent

8. The onset of sexual maturation in adolescence is known as ____.
   a. The growth spurt
   b. Maturation
   c. atrophy
   d. puberty

9. The tendency of teenagers to feel that they are always "on stage" and are constantly being judged about their appearance and their behavior is known as the _____.
   a. Personal fable
   b. Imaginary audience
   c. idealistic tendency
   d. egocentric distortion

10. According to Erikson, developing a stable sense of self and making the transition from dependence on others to dependence on oneself is called _____.
    a. Self-actualization
    b. Identity formation
    c. the personal fable
    d. identity diffusion

11. The low point of parent-child relationships usually occurs in _____.
    a. Late childhood
    b. Early adolescence
    c. mid-adolescence
    d. late adolescence

12. When adolescents are asked what they MOST dislike about themselves, they are most likely to say they dislike their _____.
    a. Personality
    b. Social status
    c. physical appearance
    d. lack of control over their life

13. Suicide is not the ____ leading cause of death among adolescents.
    a. Second
    b. Third
    c. fourth
    d. fifth

14. Couples who lived together before getting married are ___ satisfied with their marriages and ____ likely to get divorced.
    a. Less: less
    b. Less; more
    c. more; less
    d. more; more

15. The major turning point in most adults' lives is _____.
    a. Getting their first job
    b. buying their first house
    c. dealing with aging parents
    d. having and raising children

16. A time when some adults discover they nolonger feel fulfilled in their jobs or personal lives and attempt to make a decisive shift in career or lifestyle is called _____.
    a. Empty nest syndrome
    b. Midlife transition
    c. midlife crisis
    d. life review

17. The majority of older adults are _____.
    a. Impotent and incapable of sexual response
    b. Uninterested in sex
    c. Sexually active
    d. None of the above

18. Older people who were often labeled as "senile" in the past, were most likely suffering from _____.
    a. Normal aging
    b. Parkinson's disease
    c. Huntington's disease
    d. Alzheimer's disease

19. Kubler-Ross describes the sequence of stages of dying as _____.
    a. Anger, denial, depression, bargaining, acceptance
    b. Denial, anger, bargaining, depression, acceptance
    c. Denial, bargaining, depression, anger, acceptance
    d. Anger, bargaining, depression, denial, acceptance

20. Studies of teenage killers have found that most of the killers had ____ experience with guns.
    a. Virtually no
    b. Little
    c. moderate
    d. extensive

Answers and Explanations to Multiple Choice Posttest

1. c. The critical period is when certain internal and external influences have a major impact on development and little impact at other times. p. 316

2. b. Temperament refers to the physical and emotional characteristics of the newborn and infant. p. 317

3. a. Cohort refers to a group of people born during the same historical period of time. p. 314

4. c. By the end of the sensory motor stage, Piaget said most toddlers have a capacity for self-recognition and can identify "myself" in the mirror. p. 324

5. b. Abstract thinking first shows up in the formal operations stage, usually in adolescence. p. 325

6. b. The socialization process teaches children socially appropriate behaviors and attitudes. p. 332

7. b. Authoritative parents are to self reliant children as permissive parents are to dependent children. p. 332

8. d. Puberty is the onset of sexual maturation in adolescence. p. 332

9. b. The imaginary audience is the term Elkind used to describe the delusion that many adolescent's have about being constantly observed by others. p. 340

10. b. Erikson termed identity formation as the time when young people make the transition from dependence on others to self-dependency. p. 341

11. b. The low point in parent-child relationships is usually in early adolescence when physical changes are occurring. p. 342

12. c. Adolescent's tend to dislike their physical appearance more than anything else about themselves, leading to low self-esteem and possible eating disorders. p. 343

13. b. Suicide is the third leading cause of death among teens, after accidents and homicides. p. 343

14. b. Couples who cohabitated before marriage are less satisfied and more likely to divorce. They may have been more tentative about the relationship to begin with. p. 345

15. d. Having and raising children is the major turning point in most adults' lives due to increased duty, obligation, time and energy involved. p. 346

16. c. The midlife crisis is a time when some adults discover a lack of fulfillment and attempt to make a radical shift in their career or lifestyle. p. 352

17. c. The majority of older adults are sexually active. p. 356

18. d. Alzheimer's disease used to be considered rare however now it is considered what was labeled 'senile' in the past. p. 357

19. b. Kubler-Ross's five stages of accepting one's approaching death as: denial, anger. bargaining, depression and acceptance. p. 358

20. d. Killer kids were found to have extensive experience with guns and easy access to them. p. 344

Key Vocabulary Terms

Cut out each term and use as study cards.
Definition is on the back side of each term.

Developmental psychology	Prenatal development
Cross-sectional study	Fetus
Cohort	Critical period
Longitudinal study	Neonate
Biographical or retrospective study	Temperament

Development from conception to birth.	Study of the changes that occur in people from birth through old age.
A developing human between 3 months after conception and birth.	Method of studying developmental changes by comparing people of different ages at about the same time.
A time when certain internal and external influences have a major effect on development; at other periods, the same influences will have little or no effect.	Group of people born during the same period in historical time.
Newborn baby.	Method of studying developmental changes by evaluating the same people at different points in their lives.
Characteristic patterns of emotional reactions and emotional self-regulation.	Method of studying developmental changes by reconstructing people's past through interviews and inferring the effects of past events that occurred in the past on current behaviors.

Maturation	Egocentric
Sensory-motor stage	Concrete operational stage
Object permanence	Principles of conservation
Mental representation	Formal operational stage
Preoperational stage	Language acquisition device

Unable to see things from another's point of view.	Automatic biological unfolding of development in an organism as a function of the passage of time.
In Piaget's theory, the stage of cognitive development between 7 and 11 years of age, in which the individual can attend to more than one thing at a time and understand someone else's point of view.	In Piaget's theory, the stage of cognitive development between birth and 2 years, in which the individual develops object permanence and acquires the ability to form mental representations.
The concept that the quality of a substance is not altered by reversible changes in its apperance.	The concept that things continue to exist even when they are out of sight.
In Piaget's theory, the stage of cognitive development between 11 and 15 years of age, in which the individual becomes capable of abstract thought.	Mental image or symbol (such as words) used to think about or remember an object, a person, or an event.
A hypothetical neural mechanism for acquiring language that is presumed to be "wired into" all humans.	In Piaget's theory, the stage of cognitive development between 2-7 years, in which the individual becomes able to use mental representations and language to describe, remember, and reason.

Imprinting	Gender identity
Attachment	Gender constancy
Autonomy	Gender-role awareness
Socialization	Gender stereotypes
Peer group	Sex-typed behavior

A little girl's knowledge that she is a girl, and a little boy's knowledge that he is a boy.	In certain species, the tendency to follow the first moving thing (usually its mother) it sees after it is born or hatched.
The realization that gender does not change with age.	Emotional bond that develops in the first year of life that makes human babies cling to their caregivers for safety and comfort.
Knowledge of what behavior is appropriate for each gender.	Sense of independence; desire not to be controlled by others.
General beliefs about characteristics that men and women are presumed to have.	Process by which children learn the behaviors and attitudes appropriate to their family and their culture.
Socially prescribed ways of behaving that differ for boys and girls.	A network of same-aged friends and acquaintances who give one another emotional and social support.

Puberty	Clique
Menarche	Midlife crisis
Identity formation	Midlife transition
Identity crisis	Menopause
	Alzheimer's disease

Groups of adolescents with similar interests and strong mutual attachment.	The onset of sexual maturation, with accompanying physical development.
A time when adults discover they nolonger feel fulfilled in their jobs or personal lives and attempt to make a decisive shift in career or lifestyle.	First menstrual period.
According to Levinson, a process whereby adults assess the past and formulate new goals for the future.	Erikson's term for the development of a stable sense of self necessary to make the transition from dependence on others to dependence on oneself.
Time in a woman's life when menstruation ceases.	Period of intense self-examination and decision making; part of the process of identity formation.
A disorder common in late adulthood that is characterized by progressive losses in memory and changes in personality . It is believed to be caused by a deterioration of the brain's structure and function.	

10 Personality

Use this section for class and text notes. Distinguish between lecture notes, textbook concepts, topics emphasized on the exams and your own comments.

Personality

The Case of Jaylene Smith

1. Psychodynamic Theories   page 367

    A. Sigmund Freud

    - Unconscious

    - Psychoanalysis

    - How personality is structured

        – Id

        – Pleasure principle

        – Ego

        – Reality principle

        – Superego

        – Ego ideal

- How Personality Develops

  – Libido

  – Fixation

- Psychosexual Stages

  – Oral Stage

  – Anal Stage

  – Phallic Stage

- Oedipus complex

- Electra complex

  – Latency Period

  – Genital Stage

B. Carl Jung

- Personal unconscious

- Collective unconscious

- Archetypes

- Persona

- Extrovert

- Introvert

- Rational individuals

- Irrational individuals

C. Alfred Adler

- Compensation

- Inferiority complex

D. Karen Horney

- Anxiety

- Neurotic Trends

E. Eric Erikson

- 8 Stages of Development

    1. Trust vs Mistrust

    2. Autonomy vs Shame and Doubt

    3. Initiative vs Guilt

    4. Industry vs Inferiority

    5. Identity vs Role Confusion

    6. Intimacy vs Isolation

    7. Generativity vs Stagnation

    8. Ego Integrity vs Despair

F. A Psychodynamic View of Jaylene Smith

G. Evaluating Psychodynamic Theories

---

2. Humanistic Personality Theories   page 378

A. Carl Rogers

- Actualizing tendency

- Self-actualizing tendency

- Fully functioning person

- Unconditional positive regard

- Conditional positive regard

B. A Humanistic View of Jaylene Smith

C. Evaluating Humanistic Theories

3. Trait Theories p. 380

A. Personality traits

B. Factor analysis

C. Big Five

- Extroversion

- Emotional stability

- Agreeableness

- Conscientiousness

- Openness to experience

UNDERSTANDING Ourselves

The Genetic Basis of Personality Traits   page 382

D. A Trait View of Jaylene Smith

E. Evaluating Trait Theories

4. Cognitive-Social Learning Theories   page 383

A. Locus of Control and Self-Efficacy

- Cognitive-social learning theory

- Expectancies

- Locus of Control

  – Internal locus

  – External locus

- Explanatory style

- Self-efficacy

B. A Cognitive-Social Learning View of Jaylene Smith

C Evaluating Cognitive-Social Learning Theories

---

5. Personality Assessment   page 386

Reliable

Valid

Characteristic/Typical Behavior

A. The Personal Interview

- Structured

- Unstructured

B. Direct Observation

C. Objective Tests

- 16 Personality Factor Questionnaire

- NEO-PI-R

- Minnesota Multiphasic Personality Inventory (MMPI)

D. Projective Tests

- Rorschach test

- Thematic Apperception Test

Learning Objectives and Questions

After you have read and studied this chapter, you should be able to complete the following statements. Your exam is written based on these learning objectives.

OBJECTIVES

1. Define personality.

2. Summarize the interaction of elements of personality according to Freud's theory: id, ego, and superego. Identify Freud's five stages of psychosexual development.

3. Differentiate between the theories of Jung, Adler, and Horney. Identify what these theories have in common.

4. Identify Erik Erikson's eight stages of personality development.

5. Contrast Carl Rogers' humanistic theory with Freudian theory.

6. Explain trait theory.

7. List the five basic traits that most describe differences in personality.

8. Compare cognitive social-learning theories to early views of personality.

9. Describe the four basic tools psychologists use to measure personality. List two objective tests, two projective tests, and their uses.

Language Support

Students identified the following words from the text as needing more explanation. This page can be cut-out, folded in half, and used as a bookmark for this chapter.

A

Alliance	a bond or connection between people
Altercation	a noisy, heated, angry dispute
Amiable	friendly, sociable, agreeable, congenial
Amoral	lacking moral sensibility; neither moral nor immoral
Assail	attack violently with blows or words
Attain	achieve, carry out successfully, gain possession of, obtain
Autonomous	self-contained; existing independently

B

Belittle	minimize or degrade; claim something is less than it seems
Bicker	engage in a petty quarrel

C

Consensus	general agreement arrived at by most of those concerned
Constellation	gathering of related people, qualities or things; pattern or arrangement
Conviction	strong persuasion or belief or opinion
Cordially	warmly, genuinely, cheerfully or graciously
Craving	intense, urgent or abnormal desire or longing

D

Descriptors	something that describes or identifies
Disheartening	to cause to lose one's spirit or morale
Disposition	prevailing tendency, mood or inclination; temperamental makeup
Dovetail	to fit together into a whole
Drab	characterized by dullness and monotony

E

Embodied	to make concrete and perceptible; represent as a person or with human qualities
Encode	convert from one communication system to another; specify the genetic code for
Endanger	create a dangerous situation or expose to a peril

F

Fruition	realization, attainment or enjoyment of anything desired

G

Gullibility	easily deceived or cheated; naive

H

Hindsight	perception of the nature of an event after it has happened
Hostility	conflict; opposing or resisting in thought or principle; aggressive action

I

Imperatives	unavoidable obligation or requirement; absolutely necessary or required
Indebted	being obliged for a favor, owing gratitude or recognition to; owing money
Intangible	incapable of being felt, touched or discerned by the senses or mind
Intuitive	immediate knowing without apparent use of rational thought
Invisible	imperceptible by the senses or mind; subtle; hidden

J

Jock	an athlete (person active in sports); usually a college student

L

Lofty	rising to a great height; elevated in character or status

M

Magnitude	importance, quality or caliber of something; great size or extent
Mediocre	of moderate or low quality or value; ordinary, so-so
Millennia	period of 1,000 years
Mysticism	vague speculation; belief without sound basis

O

One-dimensional	shallow, superficial, lacking depth
Outbursts	violent expression or feeling; a surge of activity or growth

P

Per se	as such, essential nature; in, of, by or for itself
Proposition	proposal, something offered for consideration or acceptance
Prowess	extraordinary ability

R

Recruit	seek to enroll or enlist; newcomer to a field or activity
Redundancy	needless repetition; part of a message that can be eliminated without losing the essential meaning
Reconcile	restore friendship and harmony; resolve a disagreement
Retort	answer by a counter argument or sharp response

S

Salient	of notable significance; prominent; noticeable
Self-preservation	natural or instinctive tendency to protect one's own existence
Spawn	bring forth or generate; bring to bear; produce; bring into existence
Stifle	repress; withhold from expression; deprive of oxygen
Subordinate	lower rank or position; treat with less value or importance
Superficial	concerned with the obvious or apparent; shallow; lacking substance or depth
Surmount	overcome barriers or obstacles; surpass or exceed in accomplishment

T

Tactfully	keen sense of what is appropriate and considerate to say or do in order to maintain good relations with others or avoid offense
Tenet	principle, belief or doctrine generally held to be true
Truant	one who shirks duty; staying out of school without permission

U

Unbridled	free from restraint; spontaneous; set loose or free
Undermine	weaken gradually so as to be well established before becoming apparent

V

Vanity	inflated pride in oneself or one's appearance; conceit

W

Watchdog	one that guards against loss, waste, theft or undesirable practices

Multiple Choice Posttest

After studying the text and completing the Study Guide activities, answer these questions to determine if you need to review any areas before the course exam.

1. Which of the following is NOT an aspect of personality?
   a. Enduring
   b. Unique
   c. stable
   d. unpredictable

2. For Freud, the term "sexual instinct" refers to ____.
   a. The personal unconscious
   b. Erotic sexuality
   c. Any form of pleasure
   d. childhood experiences

3. For Freud, the only personality structure present at birth is the ___.
   a. Id
   b. Ego
   c. superego
   d. ego ideal

4. The proper chronological order of Freud's psychosexual stages is ____.
   a. Oral, anal, phallic, latency, genital
   b. Anal, oral, phallic, latency, genital
   c. Anal, oral, genital, latency, phallic
   d. Oral anal, genital, phallic, latency

5. According to Jung, the memories and behavior patterns inherited from past generations are part of the _____.
   a. Persona
   b. Alter-ego
   c. personal unconscious
   d. collective unconscious

6. Collective memories of experiences people have had in common since prehistoric times, such as mothers, heroes, or villains are called _____ by Carl Jung.
   a. Personas
   b. Celebrities' heroes
   c. archetypes
   d. collective

7. Marley is a joiner. She is interested in other people and events going on around her in the world. In Jung's view, she is an _____.
   a. Archetype
   b. Endomorph
   c. introvert
   d. extrovert

8. Adler's emphasis on people's positive social strivings has caused him to be labeled by many psychologists as the "father" of ____ psychology.
   a. Humanistic
   b. Gestalt
   c. cognitive
   d. social

9. Erikson suggested that success in each of the eight life stages he outlined depends upon _____.
   a. Resolution of the inferiority complex
   b. Cognitive and moral development
   c. Resolution of the Oedipus complex
   d. Adjustment during the previous stage

10. Erikson's stage of autonomy versus shame and doubt corresponds approximately with Freud's ____ stage of psychosexual development.
    a. oral
    b. anal
    c. phallic
    d. latency

11. Erikson argues that for people to establish as sense of intimacy, they must feel secure in their _____.
    a. Identity
    b. Initiative
    c. persona
    d. integrity

12. Studies have found that the "Big Five" dimensions of personality _____.
    a. May only represent personality in Western industrial cultures
    b. May only represent personality in North American culture
    c. May only represent personality in non-Western, non-industrial cultures
    d. May represent universal dimensions of personality across cultures

13. Each of the following is one of the "Big Five" dimensions of personality EXCEPT ____.
    a. Neuroticism
    b. Agreeableness
    c. emotional stability
    d. extroversion

14. The most widely used objective personality test is the ___.
    a. 16 PF
    b. TAT
    c. Rorschach
    d. MMPI

15. A behaviorist would prefer ____ when assessing someone's personality.
    a. Objective tests
    b. Observation
    c. Interviews
    d. Projective tests

16. The Rorschach test relies on the interpretation of ___ to understand personality.
    a. A 16-part questionnaire
    b. Cards with human figures on them
    c. 10 cards containing ink blots
    d. sentence completion exercises

17. When explaining personality, cognitive-social learning theorists put _____ at the center of personality.
    a. unconscious processes
    b. emotional stability cues
    c. mental processes
    d. environmental cues

18. Bill believes he can control his own fate. He feels that by hard work, skill and training it is possible to avoid punishments and find rewards. Rotter would say that Bill has a(n) ____ locus of control.
    a. Internal
    b. External
    c. primary
    d. secondary

19. According to Bandura, the expectancy that one's efforts will be successful is called _____.
    a. Self-esteem
    b. Locus of control
    c. self-actualizing tendency
    d. self-efficacy

20. Which of the following is NOT one of the four basic types of tools used by psychologists to measure personality?
    a. Personal interview
    b. Objective tests
    c. projective tests
    d. aptitude tests

Label Drawings

Fill-In the Blanks

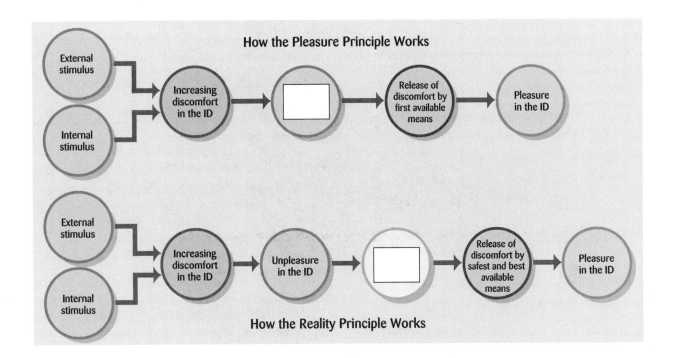

How the Pleasure Principle Works

External stimulus → Increasing discomfort in the ID → [ ] → Release of discomfort by first available means → Pleasure in the ID

Internal stimulus

External stimulus → Increasing discomfort in the ID → Unpleasure in the ID → [ ] → Release of discomfort by safest and best available means → Pleasure in the ID

Internal stimulus

How the Reality Principle Works

SUMMARY TABLE

Theories of Personality (Supply the roots of personality)

Theory	Roots of Personality	Methods of Assessing
Psychodynamic		Projective tests, personal inerviews.
Humanistic		Objective tests and personal inerviews.
Trait		Objective tests.
Social Learning Theories		Interviews, objective tests, observations.

Answers and Explanations to Multiple Choice Posttest

1. d. Unpredictability is not an aspect of personality. p. 365

2. c. For Freud, 'sexual instinct' refers to any form of pleasure. p. 368

3. a. For Freud, the id is the only personality structure present at birth. p. 368

4. a. The proper order of Freud's psychosexual stages is: oral, anal, phallic, latency, genital. p. 370

5. d. The collective unconscious consists of inherited memories and behavior patterns. p. 371

6. c. Archetypes are collective memories of common types, such as mothers and heroes. p. 371

7. d. Extroverts are interested in being with other people and in the world. p. 371

8. a. Adler is considered by many to be the "father" of humanistic psychology. p. 373

9. d. Success in Erikson's 8 life stages depends on adjustment during the previous stage. p. 374

10. b. Erikson's autonomy versus shame and doubt stage corresponds with Freud's anal stage. p. 375

11. a. For Erikson, people must feel secure in their identity to establish a sense of intimacy. p. 375

12. d. The "Big Five" dimensions of personality may represent universal dimensions across cultures. p. 382

13. a. Neuroticism is not one of the Big Five dimensions. p. 381

14. d. The MMPI is the most widely used objective personality test. p. 388

15. b. Behaviorists prefer observation when assessing personality. p. 387

16. c. The Rorschach test uses 10 cards containing inkblots. p. 389

17. c. Cognitive-social learning theorists put mental processes at the center of personality. p. 384

18. b. Bill has an external locus of control. p. 384

19. d. Self-efficacy is the expectancy that one's efforts will succeed. p. 384

20. d. Aptitude tests are not one of the 4 basic types of personality tests. p. 386–9

Label Drawings

Fill in the Blanks

Fig. 10.2 p. 369

Pleasure Principle: Unpleasure in the Id

Reality Principle: Rational thought of Ego

Summary Table p. 387

Roots of Personality

Psychodynamic: Unconscious thoughts, feelings, motives, and conflicts; repressed problem from early childhood.

Humanistic: A drive toward personal growth and higher levels of functioning.

Trait: Relatively permanent dispositions within the individual that cause the person to think, feel and act in characteristic ways.

Social Learning: Determined by past reinforcement and punishment as well as by observing what happens to other people.

Key Vocabulary Terms

Cut out each term and use as study cards.
Definition is on the back side of each term.

Personality	Pleasure principle
Psychodynamic theories	Ego
Unconscious	Reality principle
Psychoanalysis	Superego
Id	Ego ideal

According to Freud, the way in which the id seeks immediate gratification of an instinct.

An individual's unique pattern of thoughts, feelings, and behaviors that persist over time and across situations.

Freud's term for the part of the personality that mediates between environmental demands (reality), conscience (superego), and instinctual needs (id); now often used as synonym for "self."

Personality theories contending that behavior results from psychological forces that interact within the individual, often outside conscious awareness.

According to Freud, the way in which the ego seeks to satisfy instinctual demands safely and effectively in the real world.

In Freud's theory, all the ideas, thoughts, and feelings of which we are not and normally cannot become aware.

According to Freud, the social and parental standards the individual has internalized; the conscience and the ego ideal.

The theory of personality Freud developed as well as the form of therapy he invented.

The part of the superego that consists of standards of what one would like to be.

In Freud's theory of personality, the collection of unconscious urges and desires that continually seek expression.

Libido	Oedipus and Electra complexes
Fixation	Latency period
Oral stage	Genital stage
Anal stage	Personal unconscious
Phallic stage	Collective unconscious

According to Freud, a child's sexual attachment to the parent of the opposite sex and jealousy toward the parent of the same sex: generally occurs in the phallic stage.

According to Freud, the energy generated by the sexual instinct.

In Freud's theory of personality, a period in which the child appears to have no interest in the opposite sex; occurs after the phallic stage.

According to Freud, a partial or complete halt at some point in the individual's psychosexual development.

In Freud's theory of personality development, the final stage of normal adult sexual development, which is usually marked by mature sexuality.

First stage in Freud's theory of personality development in which the infant's erotic feelings center on the mouth, lips, and tongue.

In Jung's theory of personality, one of the two levels of the unconscious; it contains the individual's repressed thoughts, forgotten experiences, and undeveloped ideas.

Second stage in Freud's theory of personality development, in which a child's erotic feelings center on the anus and on elimination.

In Jung's theory of personality, the level of the unconscious that is inherited and common to all members of a species.

Third stage in Freud's theory of personality development, in which erotic feelings center on the genitals.

Archetypes	Humanistic personality theory
Persona	Actualizing tendency
Compensation	Self-actualizing tendency
Inferiority complex	Fully functioning person
Neurotic trends	Unconditional positive regard

Any personality theory that asserts the fundamental goodness of people and their striving toward higher levels of functioning.

In Jung's theory of personality, thought forms common to all human beings, stored in the collective unconscious.

According to Rogers, the drive of every organism to fulfill its biological potential and to become what it is inherently capable of becoming.

According to Jung, our public self, the mask we put on to represent ourselves to others.

According to Rogers, the drive of human beings to fulfill their self-concepts, or the images they have of themselves.

According to Adler, the person's effort to overcome imagined or real personal weaknesses.

According to Rogers, an individual whose self-concept closely resembles his or her inborn capacities or potentials.

In Adler's theory, the fixation on feelings of personal inferiority that results in emotional and social paralysis.

In Rogers' theory, the full acceptance and love of another person regardless of that person's behavior.

In Horney's theory, irrational strategies for coping with emotional problems and minimizing anxiety.

Personality traits	Locus of control
Factor analysis	Self-efficacy
Big Five	Performance standards
Cognitive-social learning theories	Objective tests
Expectancies	16 Personality Factor Questions

According to Rotter, an expectancy about whether reinforcement is under internal or external control.

Dimensions or characteristics on which people differ in distinctive ways.

According to Bandura, the expectancy that one's efforts will be successful.

A statistical technique, used by Cattell, that demonstrates that various traits tend to cluster in groups.

In Bandura's theory, standards that people develop to rate the adequacy of their own behavior in a variety of situations.

Five traits or basic dimensions currently thought to be of central importance in describing personality.

Personality tests that are administered and scored in a standard way.

Personality theories that view behavior as the product of the interaction of cognition, learning and past experiences, and the immediate environment.

Objective personality test created by Cattell that provides scores on the 16 traits he identified.

In Bandura's view, what a person anticipates in a situation or as a result of behaving in certain ways.

MMPI	Introvert
Projective tests	Conditional positive regard
Rorschach test	NEO-PI-R
Thematic Apperception Test (TAT)	
Extrovert	

According to Jung, a person who usually focuses on his or her own thoughts and feelings.	The most widely used objective personality test, originally intended for psychiatric diagnosis.
In Roger's theory, acceptance and love that are dependent on behaving in certain ways and on fulfilling certain conditions.	Personality tests, such as the Rorschach inkblot test; consisting of ambiguous or unstructured material that do not limit the response to be given.
An objective personality test designed to assess the Big Five personality traits.	A projective test composed of ambiguous inkblots, the way a person interprets the blots is thought to reveal aspects of his or her personality.
	A projective test composed of ambiguous pictures about which a person writes a complete story.
	According to Jung, a person who usually focuses on social life and the external world instead of on his or her internal experience.

11 Stress and Health Psychology

CLASS AND TEXT NOTES

Use this section for class and text notes. Distinguish between lecture notes, textbook concepts, topics emphasized on the exams and your own comments.

Adjustment

Health Psychology

1. Sources of Stress   page 397

    A. Life Changes

        • College Life Stress Inventory

    B. Everyday Hassles

    C. Pressure

    D. Frustration

        • Five Sources

            1. Delays

            2. Lack of Resources

            3. Losses

            4. Failure

            5. Discrimination

E. Conflict

- Approach/approach conflict

- Avoidance/avoidance conflict

- Approach/avoidance conflict

F. Self-imposed Stress

G. Stress and Individual Differences

- Optimists

- Pessimists

- Internal Locus of Control

- External Locus of Control

---

2. Coping with Stress   page 402

A. Direct Coping

- Confrontation

- Compromise

- Withdrawal

UNDERSTANDING Ourselves   page 404
Coping with Stress at College

B. Defensive Coping

- Defense Mechanisms

1. Denial

2. Repression

3. Projection

4. Identification

5. Regression

6. Intellectualization

7. Reaction Formation

8. Displacement

9. Sublimation

C. Socioeconomic and Gender Differences in Coping with Stress

---

3.   How Stress Affects Health   page 410

A. Selye's General Adaptation Syndrome (GAS)

- Alarm Stage

- Resistance

- Exhaustion

B. Stress and Heart Disease

- Type A

   – Chronic anger; hostility

   • Type B

C. Stress and the Immune System

   • Psychoneuroimmunology (PNI)

D. Staying Healthy

   • Calm down

   – Exercise

- Relax

   – Relaxation Training

- Reach Out

  - Social support

  - Altruism

- Learning to Cope Effectively

  - Proactive Coping

  - Positive Reappraisal

  - Humor

---

4. Sources of Extreme Stress   page 415

   A. Unemployment

   B. Divorce and separation

   C. Bereavement

   - Three Myths

   D. Catastrophes

   - Stages of Reactions

     - Suggestible Stage

     - Shock Stage

     - Recovery Stage

   E. Combat and other threatening Personal Attacks

   F. Post-Traumatic Stress Disorder

UNDERSTANDING Ourselves

Traumatic Stress: Recovering From Disasters and Other Traumatic Events   page 418–419

- Normal Responses

  – Feelings

  – Thoughts and Behavior Patterns

  – Recurring Emotional Reactions

  – Interpersonal Relationships

  – Physical Symptoms

Learning Objectives and Questions

After you have read and studied this chapter, you should be able to complete the following statements. Your exam is written based on these learning objectives.

LEARNING OBJECTIVES

1. Compare and contrast the terms stress, adjustment, pressure and frustration in terms of their causes and effects. Also describe the roles of change and hassles in contributing to stress.

2. Identify, define and discuss each of the three types of conflict described by Lewin. Discuss how people tend to react to these conflicts.

3. Summarize Kosaba's findings on hardiness, resilience and individual differences on stress.

4. Compare and contrast direct coping methods with defensive coping methods. Provide examples of each.

5. Identify, define and discuss Freud's defense mechanisms. Give one example for each defense mechanism discussed.

6. Summarize the research regarding socioeconomic and gender differences in coping with stress and discuss who experiences the most stress.

7. Explain the "flight or fight" response. Also, describe the stages of Selye's General Adaptation Syndrome pointing out relevant research.

8. Discuss the research on the relationship between stress and coronary heart disease.

9. Discuss the research on the relationship between stress and the immune system. Include information about the relationship between stress and cancer.

10. Summarize the information about the well-adjusted person. List Morris' three criterion for evaluating healthy adjustment.

11. Discuss the relatively new fields of Health Psychology and Psychoneuroimmunology and their contributions to the topic of stress and health.

ESSAY QUESTIONS

1. Discuss the role of irrational thinking on stress and how some stress is self-imposed.

2. Identify and describe five sources of extreme stress and outline some of the physical and/or psychological problems caused by each source presented. Include the 3 myths of bereavement and the three reactions to natural catastrophes.

3. Summarize the article on why some people are happier than others.

4. List the four steps for staying healthy. Detail specific suggestions for improvement and include definitions of altruism, proactive coping and positive reappraisal.

5. Define the psychological disorder, Posttraumatic Stress Syndrome. Discuss possible causes, symptoms and the 'normal' responses to a traumatic event. Include suggestions for recovery.

Language Support

Students identified the following words from the text as needing more explanation. This page can be cut-out, folded in half, and used as a bookmark for this chapter.

A

Abandon	leave without intending to return; give oneself over fully to something, withdraw support or protection
Accommodating	helpful, bring into agreement, provide with something needed, make room for, give consideration of adapt to
Adversary	having opposing interests; enemy
Aerobic exercise	sustained exercises to stimulate, strengthen and oxygenate the heart
Albeit	even though; acknowledging the fact that
Ambivalent	fluctuating between simultaneous, contradictory or opposing feelings or attitudes toward something; uncertain of which approach to take
Anniversary	yearly (annual) recurring of a date marking a notable event
Annoyance	source of irritation; nuisance; unpleasant; bothersome; disturbing

B

Blown up	built up to an unreasonable extent; expanded to reasonable proportions
Bolster	support or give a boost to; reinforce
Breakdown	failure to function, progress or be effective; classify into categories

C

Cherish	hold dear; nurture; feel or show affection for
Common denominator	a common or shared trait or theme
Component	an essential part or element
Composite	made up of distinct parts; typical or essential characteristics of a group
Congestion	clog; concentrated in a small, narrow place; something that impedes
Consumed	use up; engage or engross fully in; eat or drink in great quantity
Conventionally	based on customary conditions; lacking originality or individuality
Crass	without refinement; gross; vulgar
Cynical	distrustful of human nature and motives; pessimistic

D

Dazed	stunned, groggy, dizzy; overcome with astonishment or disbelief
Desperate	having lost hope; using extreme measure to overcome defeat; suffering extreme need or anxiety
Detonate	explode with sudden violence; set off in a burst of activity
Dissect	separate into pieces; analyze and interpret in detail or scientifically
Dissipate	to spread thin or scatter and gradually vanish
Down-sized	reduce in size; cut back (i.e., labor force); design or make smaller version
Dramatic	striking in appearance or effect; exaggerated emotionalism
Drift	general underlying meaning or tendency
Dual-earner couple	two paycheck family; both parties work and contribute to family income
Dwell	stay for a time; a resident' speak or write persistently (stay on theme)

E

Endeavor	to strive or achieve; exert effort; work with a set purpose
Endorse	approve openly, express support
Extravagantly	exceeding reasonable or necessary limits; lacking moderation, balance, restraint; excessively elaborate

F

Fatality	causing death or destruction; destined for disaster
Fatigue	weariness or exhaustion from labor, exertion or stress
Forbidden	not allowed by authorities; hinder or prevent
Free-fall	rapid and continuing drop or decline
Frozen	unable to be changed or moved; fixed; drained or incapable of emotion

G

Gracious	kind, courteous, tactful, charming, generous, with good taste
Gratifying	giving pleasure or satisfaction to; indulging
Gregarious	a liking for companionship; sociable

H

Hanging out	hang around in one's company; spend time aimlessly, loitering around
Hand-in-hand	closely associated; in cooperation with
Head-on	in direct opposition; facing forward
Hostage	one held against their will or controlled by an outside influence

I

Incompatible	not able to blend into a harmonious co-existence
Irreparable	unable to be fixed or repaired

L

Lavish	marked by excess, abundant
Looms	appear impressively great or exaggerated; take shape as an impending event

M

Mirage	an optical effect looking like water or a mirror; illusory and unattainable
Mixed blessing	having incompatible or contrary elements; both positive and negative
Mobilize	put into motion or circulation; assemble or make ready for action

N

Natural disaster	a sudden weather event bringing great damage, loss or destruction
Network	interconnected or interrelated chain, group or system
No-exit	no way or passage out; can't leave
Numb	lacking or devoid of physical sensation or emotion; indifferent

O

Obstacle	hinder or block; something that impedes progress or achievement

P

Perch	resting place or vantage point; prominent position
Petty annoyance	minor or insignificant; unimportant source of irritation, small nuisance
Preexisting	precede; exist before or earlier
Premonition	anticipate an event without conscious reason; previous notice or warning
Preponderance	excessive quantity weight, power, importance or strength
Procrastination	intentionally or habitually putting off a task; delay

Q

Queasy	causing nausea; full of doubt or uneasiness; ill at ease

R

Radical departure	set out on new course; extreme change in existing conditions or methods
Restraint	control over expression of emotions or thoughts; restrict movement
Ruminate	contemplate, reflect, ponder; go over repeatedly in thought
Rundown	item-by-item report or review; summary
Ruthless	cruel; devoid of humane feelings; causing pain or injury; aggressive

S

Substandard	below legal standards; falling short of normal quality
Suspicious	mistrust of something with evidence; mental uneasiness and uncertainty
Survivor	one who continues to function or prosper; one who remains alive

T

Terrorism	systematic use of fear tactics to dominate by force or threat
Toll	cost in life or health; extent of loss, damage or suffering
Totem pole	carved, painted pole with symbolic animal images of N.W. Indians
Transfixed	motionless; give permanent or final form; make firm, stable, stationery
Triumphant	victorious, successful; showing a sense of fulfillment and harmony
Turnover	movement of people or goods through a place; shift in personnel

U

Ubiquitous	being everywhere at the same time; widespread; constantly encountered
Unrealistic	inappropriate or not resembling reality or fact
Utterly	carried to the utmost point or highest degree; totally; absolutely

V

Vacillation	indecision; unable to take a stand; wavering between possible choices
Veterinarian	qualified doctor of animal medicine
Vicarious	enjoyed through imagined participation in another's experience

W

Winner-take-all	the victor claims the full reward
Wrestle	struggle or contend with; grapple

Multiple Choice Posttest

After studying the text and completing the Study Guide activities, answer these questions to determine if you need to review any areas before the course exam.

1. The College Life Stress Inventory (CLSI) measures _____.
   a. how much stress and change a student has undergone in a given period
   b. how effective a student's coping mechanisms are
   c. the extent to which a student has resolved stress effectively
   d. the degree to which a student's stress reaction is genetically determined

2. Henry's term paper is due and he hasn't finished it. He can turn it in unfinished and receive a failing grade or he can hand it in later and lose so many points that he will also fail. Henry's dilemma is described by Lewin as a (n) _____ conflict.
   a. approach/approach
   b. approach/avoidance
   c. avoidance/avoidance
   d. multiple approach/avoidance

3. Ken wants to go to law school but he is concerned that he will be rejected if he applies or will fail if he is admitted. Ken is faced with what Lewin calls a (n) _____ conflict.
   a. approach/approach
   b. approach/avoidance
   c. avoidance/avoidance
   d. double approach/avoidance

4. Kobasa's work on hardiness and resilience has linked people's self-confidence to _____.
   a. their sense of having some control over events
   b. their levels of intelligence
   c. adopting and internalizing traditional sex roles
   d. the tendency to be extroverted

5. Acknowledging a stressful situation directly and attempting to find a solution to the problem or attain a difficult goal is called _____.
   a. sublimation
   b. compromise
   c. confrontation
   d. aggression

6. After weeks of being taunted by her so-called "friends" at school, Alyssa begins actively avoiding them whenever possible. Her coping style is best described as _____.
   a. confrontation
   b. withdrawal
   c. compromise
   d. rationalization

7. John refuses to admit he has a problem with procrastination, even though his procrastination is creating many problems in his life. John is using ____ to cope with his problem.
   a. denial
   b. sublimation
   c. repression
   d. intellectualization

8. A corporate executive who feels guilty about the way she rose to power accuses her colleagues of ruthless ambition. Her behavior typifies _____.
   a. sublimation
   b. projection
   c. displacement
   d. identification

9. A student, angry that he failed what he felt was an unfair test, goes back to his dormitory and slams the door violently. This student is using the defense mechanism of ____.
   a. sublimation
   b. reaction formation
   c. projection
   d. displacement

10. The proper order in which Selye's stages of the General Adaptation Syndrome (GAS) occur is _____.
    a. resistance, alarm stage, exhaustion
    b. exhaustion, resistance, alarm stage
    c. resistance, exhaustion, alarm stage
    d. alarm stage, resistance, exhaustion

11. People who respond to life events in an intense, time urgent manner are exhibiting a _____ behavior pattern.
    a. Type A
    b. Type B
    c. Type C
    d. hyperactive

2. Prolonged stress has _____ cancer.
    a. been shown to decrease vulnerability to
    b. been found to be unrelated to one's vulnerability to
    c. been shown to increase vulnerability to
    d. been shown to cause

13. When recent or past highly stressful events result in anxiety, sleeplessness, and nightmares, a psychological disorder called _____ might be occurring.
    a. generalized anxiety disorder
    b. panic disorder
    c. posttraumatic stress disorder
    d. panic disorder

14. Which of the following accurately lists in order the stages of reactions to natural catastrophes?
    a. suggestible stage, shock stage, recovery stage
    b. shock stage, suggestible stage, recovery stage
    c. rage, confusion, recovery
    d. confusion, rage, recovery

15. Kobasa described hardiness as a trait in which _____.
    a. our experience of stress is affected by heredity
    b. people adhere to rigid actions and won't compromise
    c. people react to conflict in a hard way
    d. people experience difficult environmental demands as challenging rather than threatening

16. When people are well-adjusted they probably have ____.
    a. learned to get what they need regardless of what others want
    b. learned to balance conformity and nonconformity as well as self-control and spontaneity
    c. few problems
    d. none of the above

Answers and Explanations to Multiple Choice Posttest

1. a.   The CLSI measures how much stress and change a student has undergone in a given period. p. 397–8

2. c.   Henry's dilemma is an avoidance/avoidance conflict because both outcomes are undesirable. p. 400

3. b.   Ken is faced with an approach/avoidance conflict because he is both attracted to and repelled from his goals. p. 400

4. a.   Kosaba links people's self confidence to their sense of having some control over events. p. 401

5. c.   Confrontation acknowledges a stressful situation directly and attempting to find a solution. p. 403

6. b.   Alyssa is using the coping style of withdrawal by avoiding the situation. p. 405

7. a.   John is using denial by refusing to acknowledge his problems with procrastination. p. 405

8. b.   The female executive is using projection by attributing her repressed guilt about her success to her colleagues. p. 406

9. d.   The student is using displacement by redirecting his anger to a substitute object. p. 406–7

10. d.   The proper order in Seyle's stages of GAS are: alarm; resistance, exhaustion. p. 410–11

11. a.   One characteristic of the Type A personality is intense time urgency. p. 411–12

12. c.   Prolonged stress has been shown to increase vulnerability to cancer. p. 412

13. c.   Posttraumatic stress disorder is characterized by episodes of anxiety, sleeplessness, and nightmares resulting from a disturbing past event. p. 417–20

14. b.   The order of the states of reaction to natural catastrophes is: stage, suggestible and recovery. p. 416

15. d.   Hardiness is described as a train in which people experience difficult environmental demands as challenging rather than threatening. p. 401

16. b.   Well-adjusted people have learned to balance conformity and nonconformity as well as self-control and spontaneity. p. 420

Cut out each term and use as study cards.
Definition is on the back side of each term.

Stress	Conflict
Adjustment	Approach/ approach conflict
Health psychology	Avoidance/ avoidance conflict
Pressure	Approach/ avoidance conflict
Frustration	Confrontation

Simultaneous existence of incompatible demands, opportunities, needs, or goals.	A state of psychological tension or strain or any environmental demand that creates a state of tension or threat and requires change or adaptation.
According to Lewin the result of simultaneous attraction to two appealing possibilities, neither of which has any negative qualities.	Any effort to cope with stress.
According to Lewin, the result of facing a choice between two undesirable possibilities, neither of which has any positive qualities.	A subfield of psychology concerned with the relationship between psychological factors and physical health and illness.
According to Lewin, the result of being simultaneously attracted to and repelled by the same goal.	A feeling that one must speed up, intensify, or change the direction of one's behavior or live up to a higher standard of performance.
Acknowledging a stressful situation directly and attempting to find a solution to the problem or attain the difficult goal.	The feeling that occurs when a person is prevented from reaching a goal.

Compromise	Projection
Withdrawal	Identification
Defense mechanisms	Regression
Denial	Intellectualization
Repression	Reaction formation

Attributing one's own repressed motives, feelings, or wishes to others.	Deciding on a more realistic solution or goal when an ideal solution or goal is not practical.
Taking on the characteristics of someone else to avoid feeling incompetent.	Avoiding a situation when other forms of coping are not practical.
Reverting to childlike behavior and defenses.	Self-deceptive techniques for reducing stress, including denial, repression, projection, identification, regression, intellectualization, reaction formation, displacement, and sublimation.
Thinking abstractly about stressful problems as a way of detaching oneself from the problem.	Refusal to acknowledge a painful or threatening reality or not experiencing fully the intensity of the event.
Expression of exaggerated ideas and emotions that are the opposite of one's repressed beliefs or feelings.	Excluding uncomfortable thoughts, feelings, and desires from consciousness.

Displacement	
Sublimation	
General adaptation syndrome	
Psychoneuro-immunology	
Posttraumatic stress disorder	

	Shifting repressed motives and emotions from an original object to a substitute object.
	Redirecting repressed motives and feelings into more socially acceptable channels.
	According to Selye, the three stages the body passes through as it adapts to stress: alarm reaction, resistance, and exhaustion.
	A new field of medicine that studies the interaction between stress on the one hand and immune, endocrine, and nervous system activity on the other.
	Psychological disorder characterized by episodes of anxiety, sleeplessness, and nightmares resulting from some disturbing past event.

12 Psychological Disorders

C L A S S   A N D   T E X T   N O T E S

Use this section for class and text notes. Distinguish between lecture notes, textbook concepts, topics emphasized on the exams and your own comments.

1. Perspectives on Psychological Disorders   page 427

    A. Historical Views of Psychological Disorders

    B. The Biological Model

    C. The Psychoanalytic Model

    D. The Cognitive-Behavioral Method

    E. The Diathesis-Stress Model and Systems Theory

        •   Diathesis

        •   Biopsychosocial model

    F. Classifying Abnormal Behavior

        •   Diagnostic and Statistical Manual of Mental Disorders (DSM-IV)

    G. The Prevalence of Psychological Disorders

2. Mood Disorders   page 432

   A. Depression

      • Clinical Depression

      • Major Depressive Disorder

      • Dysthymia

   B. Suicide

   C. Mania and Bipolar Disorder

   D. Causes of Mood Disorders

      • Biological factors

      • Psychological factors

      • Social factors

UNDERSTANDING Ourselves   page 434

Recognizing Depression

      • DSM Symptoms

---

3. Anxiety Disorders page   437

   A. Specific Phobias

      • Social phobia

      • Agoraphobia

   B. Panic Disorders

   C. Other Anxiety Disorders

      • Generalized anxiety disorder

      • Obsessive-compulsive disorder (OCD)

- Acute stress disorder

- Posttraumatic stress disorder

D. Causes of Anxiety Disorders

---

4. Psychosomatic and Somatoform Disorders   page 441

A. Psychosomatic Disorder

B. Somatoform Disorders

C. Conversion Disorders

D. Hypochondriasis

E. Body Dysmorphic Disorder

---

5. Dissociative Disorders   page 443

A. Dissociative Amnesia

B. Dissociative Fugue

C. Dissociative Identity Disorder

- Multiple Personality Disorder

D. Depersonalization Disorder

---

6. Sexual and Gender-Identity Disorders   page 445

A. Sexual Dysfunction

- Erectile Disorder (ED)

- Female Sexual Arousal Disorder

B. Paraphilias

- Fetishism

- Pedophilia

C. Gender-Identity Disorders

- Gender-Identity Disorders in Children

The Insanity Defense

Learning Objectives and Questions

After you have read and studied this chapter, you should be able to complete the following statements. Your exam is written based on these learning objectives.

OBJECTIVES

1. Distinguish among the standards for defining abnormal behavior from the view of society, the individual, and the mental health professional.

2. Summarize historical attitudes toward abnormal behavior.

3. State the four current models of abnormal behavior and explain the diathesis-stress model. Explain how the DSM-IV classifies mental disorders.

4. Distinguish between the two basic kinds of mood disorders and how they may interact with each other.

5. Describe the differences between depression and a normal reaction to negative life events.

6. Discuss the possible causes of mood disorders including biological and psychological factors.

7. Describe the anxiety disorders.

8. Describe the characteristics of the psychophysiological disorders and the somatoform disorders.

9. Characterize three different types of dissociative disorders.

10. Define and give examples of the sexual disorders.

11. Define gender-identity disorders.

12. Define personality disorders. Describe four kinds of personality disorders.

13. Describe four types of schizophrenic disorders and identify possible causes of the disorder.

14. Discuss Attention-deficit/hyperactivity disorder (ADHD).

15. Discuss the complex factors that contribute to different rates of abnormal behavior in men and women.

Language Support

Students identified the following words from the text as needing more explanation. This page can be cut-out, folded in half, and used as a bookmark for this chapter.

A

Alienated	withdrawn or diverted; unfriendly or hostile with a former attachment; estranged
Ambitious	having a desire to achieve a particular goal; aspiring
Animated	full of movement, activity, spirit; lively
Apathetic	having or showing little or no feeling or emotion; indifferent
Apprehensive	anxiety or alarm about the future; showing quick insight or understanding
Arrested	bring to a stop; make inactive

B

"The blues"	low spirits; melancholy, sad

C

Causative	operating or effective as a cause or agent
Chastity	abstaining from sexual intercourse; pure intention and conduct; personal integrity
Coexist	live in peace with each other; exist together at the same time
Cold-blooded	emotionless; acting without consideration or mercy; matter of fact
Con man	swindler; person who robs others after gaining their trust

D

Debilitating	impaired strength; weaken or reduce in intensity or effectiveness; crippling or disabling; loss of health of power
Definitive	final solution or ending; solution; serving as a perfect example
Deviance	stray from a standard, principle or topic; depart from established norms
Devious	deceptive; deliberately leading astray into mistaken belief, action or direction
Dismaying	at a loss as to how to deal with something; loss of courage due to pressure, fear or anxiety
Disobedient	refusing to follow directions or guidance; refuse to conform or comply with
Disparage	degrade; speak slightingly about; demote or lower rank or reputation
Distress	mentally or emotionally worried or troubled; make ill or cause a physical disorder in
Dubious	doubtful; causing uncertainty; questionable or suspect as to true nature or quality

E

Eccentric	deviating from established style; unconventional; strange
Entitlement	having grounds for seeking or claiming something
Erratic	lack of consistency, regularity or uniformity; having no fixed course
Euphoria	feeling of well being or elation; high spirits
Exemplify	embody; be typical of or represent; serve as an example
Exorcism	act of removing or expelling something menacing or troublesome
Exploit	to use unfairly for one's own advantage

F

Facsimile	exact copy, reproduction, duplicate
Fake	something that is not what it seems to be; worthless imitation

Fanciful	unrestrained imagination lacking factual reality
Feign	give false appearance; pretend; assert as if true
Fidgety	uneasiness or restlessness shown by nervous movements
"In a Fog"	in a state of mental confusion or unawareness; in a daze
Fragile	easily broken or destroyed; delicate; lacking physical vigor
Frantic	emotionally out of control, marked by fast and nervous, disordered or anxiety driven activity
Fruitful	great resourcefulness of thought or imagination; abundant possibilities for development
Full-blown	having attained complete status; fully developed or mature

G

Genuine	sincerely and honestly felt or experiences; sincere, true, authentic
Gesture	movement or position of body or part of body that expresses an idea, opinion or emotion
"Get off"	to experience with great pleasure
Grandiose	absurd exaggerations; grand display
Grimace	a facial expression usually of disgust or disapproval

H

Horrifying	feel shock, distaste; to distress greatly
Hot line	direct phone line constantly available to the public for some specific purpose
Humiliating	extremely destructive to one's self respect or dignity
Hyper vigilance	excessively watchful, especially to danger

I

Ideology	systematic body of concepts and theories, usually about human life or culture
Impassive	no sign or feeling of emotion, pain or physical feeling, expressionless
Inappropriate	not suitable or compatible with
Incoherence	unintelligible, lacking clarity, order, cohesion or relevance
Incompetence	inadequate or unsuitable for a particular purpose; lacking the qualities needed for the effective action
Incomprehensible	impossible to understand
Intended	have in mind a purpose or goal; direct the mind on a future plan
Invulnerable	incapable of being injured or harmed; immune to attack

J

| Jargon | the language of a particular trade, profession or group |
| Jittery | continuous, fast repetitive movements; to be nervous or act nervously |

L

| Lethal | gravely damaging or destructive; capable of causing death |
| Lifestyle | typical way of life of an individual, group or culture reflecting attitudes and preference |

M

Maladaptive	unable to adjust or fit
Malfunction	fail to operate normally
Mannerisms	characteristic, often unconscious actions that may be exaggerated or affected
Melancholy	depressed spirits, dejected, sad mood
Misconception	to interpret incorrectly, misunderstand
Momentum	driving force; strength gained by motion or through the development of events
Mutually exclusive	relationship where the presence of one factor prevents the appearance of the other

N

Nurture — to foster the development of; provide with nourishment

O

Onset — the point at which something begins; early stage or period

P

Painstakingly — extremely careful or precise about details; making great effort

"Possessed" — influenced or controlled by something, such as an evil spirit or passion

Promiscuity — having numerous casual sexual partners; indiscriminate

Q

Qualitative — relating to or involving the quality or kind

R

Rat race — exhausting and usually competitive routine activity

Readily — without hesitation; willing; easily

Revert — go back to a former habit, action or belief; go back in thought or discussion

Rival gang — competing group of people usually involving criminal behavior

Robot-like — an efficient, insensitive person who functions automatically; human-like machine that performs complex human actions

S

Savagely — enraged or furiously angry; fierce or cruel person; criticize or assault brutally

Scarcity — lack of provisions for the support of life

Scheming — making sly and underhanded plans; calculating; devious

Spectrum — continuous or connected sequence, series or range

Stew — state of suppressed agitation, worry or resentment

Stewardess — female airline flight attendant

Sweeping conclusions — outcome or final result with wide range or force

T

Theoretical — existing only in theory, not practical; speculative

Timid — lacking courage, confidence, boldness or determination; shy

Tiptoe — strain upwards, on balls of feet and toes or tips of toes; moving secretly

Tyrannical — unjustly cruel or severe; oppressive; exerting absolute power or control

U

Ugliness — offensive or unpleasant to the sight

Unconventional — not bound by established customs; out of the ordinary

V

Vague — indefinite; not clearly expressing one's thoughts or feelings; hazy

Venture — an undertaking involving chance, risk or danger

Vignette — short, descriptive literary sketch; brief incident

Vindictiveness — intending to seek revenge; causing anguish or hurt; spiteful

W

Wild — strongly passionate, emotion or eager; marked by turbulent agitation; without regulation or control; off an intended course

Wrenching — causing mental or emotional anguish

Multiple Choice Posttest

After studying the text and completing the Study Guide activities, answer these questions to determine if you need to review any areas before the course exam.

1. The person whose naturalistic views of mental illness first encouraged a system search to uncover its causes, and implied that disturbed people should be treated with care and sympathy was _____.
   a. Hippocrates
   b. Galen
   c. Voltaire
   d. Descartes

2. The turning point year in the history of treatment of the mentally ill was _____, when Phillipe Pinel became director of the Bicetre Hospital in Paris and argued for pleasant living conditions for the patients.
   a. 1379
   b. 1793
   c. 1894
   d. 1937

3. The basic reason for the failed, and sometimes abusive, treatment of mentally disturbed people throughout history has been _____.
   a. Fear of retribution by supernatural forces
   b. A lack of understanding of the causes and treatments of psychological disorders
   c. Political and legal restrictions placed on treatment by insensitive authorities.
   d. Lack of money to provide adequate care for disturbed people.

4. The _____ model of mental illness holds that abnormal behavior is caused by physiological malfunction that is often attributable to hereditary factors.
   a. Biological
   b. Cognitive-behavioral
   c. Psycho-dynamic
   d. Naturalistic

5. The view that people biologically predisposed to a mental disorder will tend to exhibit that acute stress disorder when particularly affected by stress is known as the _____ model of abnormal behavior.
   a. Multimodal
   b. Pluralistic model
   c. Psychoneuro-immunological
   d. Diathesis-stress

6. The _____ model believes that fears, depression and self-defeating beliefs are caused by learning and negative thinking and can be unlearned with appropriate reinforcement.
   a. Biological
   b. Cognitive-behavioral
   c. Psycho-analytic
   d. Diathesis-stress

7. An affective/mood disorder that includes both depression and mania is known as ____.
   a. Histrionic
   b. Bipolar
   c. Dual process
   d. Obsessive-compulsive

8. An intense, paralyzing fear of a specific situation, object, person, or thing in the absence of any real danger is a ____.
   a. panic disorder
   b. phobic disorder
   c. conversion disorder
   d. compulsive disorder

9. An anxiety disorder in which a person feels driven to think disturbing thought and/or to perform senseless rituals is ____ disorder.
   a. Obsessive-compulsive
   b. Delusional-compulsive
   c. Passive-aggressive
   d. Diathesis stress

10. Mental disorders are categorized according to ___ in the DSM-IV.
    a. family histories
    b. biological causes of disruptive behavior
    c. significant behavior patterns
    d. specific theoretical approaches

11. The disorder previously known as "multiple personality disorder" is now known as

_____.
   a. Dissociative amnesia
   b. Dissociative identity disorder
   c. Dissociative fugue
   d. Depersonalization disorder

12. The most widely accepted explanation for dissociative identity disorder is that it is a response to _____.
   a. neurotransmitter imbalances
   b. childhood abuse
   c. role diffusion
   d. extreme loneliness

13. Sexual arousal as a result of fantasizing about or engaging in sexual activity with prepubescent children is _____.
   a. Infantile sexual regression
   b. Sadomasochistic immaturity
   c. Pedophilia
   d. Transvestism

14. Rejection of one's biological gender and persistently desiring to become a member of the opposite sex is known as _____.
   a. Sexual orientation disorder
   b. Bisexuality
   c. Gender identity disorder
   d. Hermaphroditism

15. John is a pathological liar. He takes things from others, takes advantage of them and never exhibits any remorse after he is done. John has ____ personality disorder.
   a. Paranoid
   b. Narcissistic
   c. Antisocial
   d. Borderline

16. _____ disorders are marked by disordered communication and thoughts, inappropriate emotions and bizarre behaviors.
   a. Psychosexual
   b. Neurotic
   c. Somatoform
   d. Schizophrenic

17. The psychological term for someone who is mentally disturbed to the point of not being in contact with reality and not being legally responsible for his or her action is ____.
   a. Schizophrenia
   b. Split personality
   c. Insanity
   d. Psychopathology

18. Research suggests that a biological vulnerability to schizophrenia may lie in excess amounts of ____.
   a. Thyroxin
   b. Epinephrine
   c. Vasopressin
   d. Dopamine

19. Currently the cause of attention deficit/hyperactivity disorder and autism is thought to be ____.
   a. arrested emotional development
   b. biological and/or genetic abnormalities
   c. over-demanding and emotionally detached parents
   d. prenatal maternal alcohol use

20. Women are more likely to suffer from ____than men and men are more likely to suffer from _____ than women.
   a. depression, substance abuse disorders
   b. antisocial personality; anxiety disorder
   c. substance abuse disorders; depression
   d. paranoid disorders; histrionic disorders

Answers and Explanations to
Multiple Choice Posttest

1. a. Hippocrates maintained that mental illness was a natural event arising from natural causes and should be treated the same as people with physical illnesses. p. 429

2. b. In 1793, Philippe Pinel was made Director of the Bicetre Hospital in Paris and drastically reorganize the care and treatment for the mentally ill. p. 429

3. b. Lack of understanding of the nature and causes of psychological disorders is the basic reason for the failed and sometimes abusive treatment of the mentally ill. p. 429

4. a. The biological model holds that psychological disorders have a biochemical or physiological basis. p. 430

5. d. The diathesis-stress model sees people who are biologically predisposed to a mental disorder will exhibit that disorder when affected by extreme stress. p. 431

6. b. Bipolar disorder alternates between periods of mania and depression, along with period of normal moods. p. 436

7. a. Phobic disorders are characterized by an intense, paralyzing, and irrational fear of something. p. 438

8. a. A person with obsessive/compulsive disorder feels driven to think disturbing thoughts or to perform senseless rituals to reduce anxiety. p. 439

9. b. The cognitive-behavioral model views psychological disorders as resulting from learning maladaptive ways of thinking and behaving. p. 430

10. c. The DSM-IV lists mental disorders in terms of significant behavior patterns. p. 431

11. b. Dissociative Identity Disorder was formerly called Multiple Personality Disorder. p. 443

12. b. Clinicians report a history of child abuse in more than 3/4 of their Dissociative identity disorder cases. p. 444

13. c. Pedophilia is the desire to have sexual relationships with children. p. 446

14. c. Gender Identity Disorder is the desire to become a member of the other biological sex. p. 446

15. c. Some individual with Antisocial Personality Disorder lie, steal, cheat and show little or no sense of responsibility or remorse. p. 447

16. d. Schizophrenia is marked by disordered communications and thoughts and inappropriate emotions and bizarre behavior. p. 449–452

17. c. Insanity is a legal term for mentally disturbed people not considered responsible for their criminal actions. p. 450

18. d. Recent research suggests the schizophrenia may be related to excessive amounts of dopamine in the central nervous system. p. 452

19. b. We don't yet know the cause of either ADHD or autism, but most theorists believe that they result almost entirely from biological or genetic factors. p. 453–4

20. a. Men drink or abuse drugs more when they have psychological problems and women are more likely to become depressed and helpless. p. 455

Key Vocabulary Terms

Cut out each term and use as study cards.
Definition is on the back side of each term.

Biological model of psychological disorders	Systems approach of psychological disorders
Psychoanalytic model of psychological disorders	Mood disorders
Cognitive-behavioral model of psychological disorders	Depression
Diathesis-stress model of psychological disorders	Mania
Diathesis	Bipolar disorder

View that biological, psychological, and social risk factors combine to produce psychological disorders. Also known as the biopsychosocial model of psychological disorders.	View that psychological disorders have a biochemical or physiological basis.
Disturbances in mood or prolonged emotional state.	View that psychological disorders are the result from unconscious internal conflicts.
A mood disorder characterized by overwhelming feelings of sadness, lack of interest in activities, and perhaps excessive guilt or feelings of worthlessness.	View that psychological disorders result from learning maladaptive ways of thinking and behaving.
A mood disorder characterized by euphoric states, extreme physical activity, excessive talkativeness, distractedness, and sometimes grandiosity.	View that people biologically predisposed to a mental disorder (those with a certain diathesis) will tend to exhibit that disorder when particularly affected by stress.
A mood disorder in which periods of mania and depression alternate, sometimes with periods of normal mood intervening.	Biological predisposition.

Cognitive distortions	Panic disorder
Anxiety disorders	Generalized anxiety disorder
Specific phobia	Obsessive-compulsive disorder
Social phobia	Psychosomatic disorders
Agoraphobia	Somatoform disorders

An anxiety disorder characterized by recurrent panic attacks in which the person suddenly experiences intense fear or terror without any reasonable cause.

A maladaptive response to early negative life events that leads to feelings of incompetence and unworthiness that are reactivated whenever a new situation arises that resembles the original events.

An anxiety disorder characterized by prolonged vague but intense fears that are not attached to any particular object or circumstance.

Disorders in which anxiety is a characteristic feature or the avoidance of anxiety seems to motivate abnormal behavior.

An anxiety disorder in which a person feels driven to think disturbing thoughts and/or to perform senseless rituals.

Anxiety disorder characterized by an intense, paralyzing fear of something.

Disorders in which there is real physical illness that is largely caused by psychological factors such as stress and anxiety.

An anxiety disorder characterized by excessive, inappropriate fears connected with social situations or performances in front of other people.

Disorders in which there is an apparent physical illness for which there is no organic basis.

An anxiety disorder that involves multiple, intense fear of crowds, public places, and other situations that require separation from a source of security such as the home.

Conversion disorders	Dissociative Identity Disorder
Hypochondriasis	Sexual dysfunction
Body dysmorphic disorder	Paraphilias
Dissociative disorders	Fetishism
Depersonalization disorder	Pedophilia

(Multiple Personality Disorder) Disorder characterized by the separation of the personality in to two or more distinct personalities.

Somatoform disorders in which a dramatic specific disability has no physical cause but instead seems related to psychological problems.

Loss or impairment of the ordinary physical responses of sexual function.

A somatoform disorder in which a person interprets insignificant symptoms as signs of serious illness in the absence of any organic evidence of such illness.

Sexual disorders in which unconventional objects or situations cause sexual arousal.

A somatoform disorder in which a person becomes so preoccupied with his or her imagined ugliness that normal life is impossible.

A paraphilia in which a nonhuman object is the preferred or exclusive method of achieving sexual excitement.

Disorders in which some aspect of the personality seems separated from the rest.

Desire to have sexual relations with children as the preferred or exclusive method of achieving sexual excitement.

A dissociative disorder whose essential feature is that the person suddenly feels changed or different in a strange way.

Gender-identity disorders	Dependent personality disorder
Gender-identity disorder in children	Avoidant personality disorder
Personality disorders	Narcissistic personality disorder
Schizoid personality disorder	Borderline personality disorder
Paranoid personality disorder	Antisocial personality disorder

Personality disorder in which the person is unable to make choices and decisions independently and cannot tolerate being alone.	Disorders that involve the desire to become, or the insistence that one really is, a member of the other biological sex.
Personality disorder in which the person's fears of rejection by others lead to social isolation.	Rejection of one's biological gender in childhood, along with the clothing and behavior that society considers appropriate to that gender.
Personality disorder in which the person has an exaggerated sense of self-importance and needs constant admiration.	Disorders in which inflexible and maladaptive ways of thinking and behaving learned early in life cause distress to the person or conflicts with others.
Personality disorder characterized by marked instability in self-image, mood, and interpersonal relationships.	Personality disorder in which a person is withdrawn and lacks feelings for others.
Personality disorder that involves a pattern of violent, criminal, or unethical and exploitative behavior and an inability to feel affection for others.	Personality disorder in which the person is inappropriately suspicious and mistrustful of others.

Schizophrenic disorders	Disorganized schizophrenia
Psychotic (Psychosis)	Catatonic schizophrenia
Insanity	Paranoid schizophrenia
Hallucinations	Undifferentiated schizophrenia
Delusions	Attention-deficit/ hyperactivity disorder (ADHD)

Schizophrenic disorder in which bizarre and childlike behaviors are common.

Severe disorder in which there are disturbances of thoughts, communications, and emotions, including delusions and hallucinations.

Schizophrenic disorder in which disturbed motor behavior is prominent.

Behavior characterized by a loss of touch with reality.

Schizophrenic disorder marked by extreme suspiciousness and complex, bizarre delusions.

Legal term for mentally disturbed people who are not considered responsible for their criminal actions.

Schizophrenic disorder in which there are clear schizophrenic symptoms that don't meet the criteria for another subtype of the disorder.

Sensory experiences in the absence of external stimulation.

A childhood disorder characterized by inattention, impulsiveness, and hyperactivity.

False beliefs about reality that have no basis in fact.

Autistic disorder

A childhood disorder
characterized by lack of
social instincts and
strange motor behavior.

13 Therapies

Use this section for class and text notes. Distinguish between lecture notes, textbook concepts, topics emphasized on the exams and your own comments.

1. Insight Therapies   page 461

    A. Psychoanalysis

        • Sigmund Freud

        • Free association

        • Transference

        • Insight

    B. Client Centered (Person-Centered) Therapy

        • Carl Rogers

        • Unconditional positive regard

        • Nondirective

C. Gestalt Therapy

- Fritz Perls

- Encounter groups

  – Empty chair technique

D. Recent Developments

- Short-term psychodynamic therapy

  – Immediate problems

---

2. Behavior Therapies   page 467

A. Using Classical Conditioning Techniques

- Desensitization, Extinction and Flooding

  – systematic desensitization

  – hierarchy of fears

- Extinction

- Flooding

- Aversive conditioning

B. Therapies Based on Operant Conditioning

- Behavior contracting

- Token economy

C. Therapies Based on Modeling

- Modeling

---

3.   Cognitive Therapies   page 470

Cognitive Behavior Therapists

A. Stress-Inoculation Therapy

B. Rational-Emotive Therapy

- Albert Ellis

C. Beck's Cognitive Therapy

---

4.   Group Therapies   page 473

A. Self-Help Groups

B. Family Therapy

C. Couple Therapy

- Empathy training

UNDERSTANDING Ourselves   page 474–5

How to Find Help

---

5.   Effectiveness of Psychotherapy   page 476

A. Therapist Alliance

B. Eclecticism

6. Biological Treatments   page 478

   A. Drug Therapies

      • Antipsychotic drugs

      • Antidepressant drugs

      • Lithium

      • Other medications

         – Psychostimulants

         – Antianxiety medications

         – Sedatives

         – Antidepressant medications

   B. Electroconvulsive Therapy (ECT)

      • Unilateral ECT

   C. Psychosurgery

      • Prefrontal lobotomy

---

7. Caring for the Seriously Disturbed and Preventing Disorders   page 483

   A. Past treatment

   B. Deinstitutionalization

   C. Alternative Forms of Treatment

   D. Prevention

   • Primary prevention

   • Secondary prevention

   • Tertiary prevention

Learning Objectives and Questions

After you have read and studied this chapter, you should be able to complete the following statements. Your exam is written based on these learning objectives.

OBJECTIVES

1. Differentiate between insight therapies, behavior therapies, cognitive therapies, and group therapies.

2. Discuss the criticisms of psychoanalysis.

3. Explain how client-centered and rational-emotive therapists interpret causes of emotional problems. Describe the therapeutic techniques of these approaches.

4. Summarize the behavioral therapist's interpretation of disorders. Describe aversive conditioning, desensitization, and modeling.

5. Describe stress-inoculation therapy, Beck's cognitive therapy, and Gestalt therapy.

6. List the advantages and disadvantages of group therapies. Identify five current approaches to group therapy.

7. Discuss the effectiveness of insight therapy and behavior therapy.

8. Outline the available biological treatments and discuss the advantages and disadvantages of each.

9. Summarize the inadequacies of institutionalization. List the alternative to institutionalization.

10. Explain the differences between primary, secondary, and tertiary prevention.

11. Discuss gender and cultural differences in relationship to treatment of psychological problems.

Language Support

Students identified the following words from the text as needing more explanation. This page can be cut-out, folded in half, and used as a bookmark for this chapter.

A

Accurate	correct; free from error; conforming exactly to truth or a standard
Advent	coming into being or use
Ambulatory	capable of moving from place to place; not bedridden
Aspiring	seeking to attain or accomplish a particular goal

C

Cardinal rule	the most important principle or procedure
Clam up	to become silent
Common sense	sound and wise but unsophisticated judgment; unreflective opinions of ordinary people
Constrictions	inhibit, prohibit or discourage spontaneous activity; restrain

D

Debilitating	weaken; impair the strength of; reduce in intensive or effectiveness
Demoralized	weaken the morale; discourage; upset the normal function
Derogatory	speak poorly of; degrade; lower rank or reputation
Dialogue	conversation between two or more people; an exchange of ideas and opinions
Dire	disastrous; extreme; desperately urgent
Discharge	release from confinement, custody or care
Discount	to minimize the importance of; view with doubt
Disproportionate	mismatch; disparity or lack of balance or relationship with
Doomed	to make certain something fails; to fix the fate of
Duration	time during which something exists or continues

E

Edgewise	sideways; with one edge pointed forward
Engaged	having attention occupied; busy; greatly interested in activity; interlock
Emphatically	emphasize; express forcefully in speech or decisive action
Entrench	establish solidly; place self in strong defensive position
Enviable	highly desirable
Erroneous	wrong; straying from truth; containing errors
Escalate	increase in extent, volume, number, amount or scope; expand
Exemplify	serve as an example; embody; typify; make concrete and perceptible

F

Face to face	in direct contact or confrontation; in each other's sight or presence
Feasible	capable of being carried out successfully; likely; doable
Fraught	filled with or accompanied by something specific; emotional distress or tension

H

Halfway house	residence for formerly institutionalized people as they transition to private life
Herald	signal the approach of; greed with enthusiasm or announce
Hodgepodge	jumble; mixture of parts of different elements
Hostel	supervised lodging usually for young travelers

I

Inconsistent	behavior or standards that aren't in agreement
Infantile	very immature; characteristic of an infant
Inhibit	discourage from free or spontaneous activity often through inner psychological impediments or social controls
Intractable	not easily managed, relieved, cured or removed

L

Last resort	final source of help or protection
Loathsome	disgusting, repulsive or having an aversion to
Lurk	waiting in a concealed place suggesting an evil purpose

M

Magnify	increase or intensify in significance; enlarge
Makeshift	usually crude and temporary substitute as a means to an end
Masquerade	acting or appearing as mere disguise or show
Meek	submissive or compliant, humbly patient
Mere	nothing more nor better than what something is; only
Modality	form of treatment with certain conditions for implementation
Money-grubber	preoccupied with making and accumulating money
Monopolize	assume complete possession or control of
Morbid	unhealthy mental attitude; excessively gloomy; horrified or intensely afraid

O

Overbearing	domineering; of overwhelming or critical importance; rudely arrogant

P

Penny wise/pound foolish	careful in dealing with small matters and reckless in dealing with important matters
Perverse	corrupt; willfully determined not to do what is expected or desired
Predicament	difficult or trying situation
Prey	helpless or unable to resist attack; victim
Proliferate	increase in number or spread rapidly; multiply

R

Rebuttal	to refute; expose falseness of; contradict or oppose; offer opposing data
Refugee	a person who flees to a foreign country to escape danger or persecution
Restore	put back into use or former or original state; renew
Revelation	striking disclosure; something communicated or discussed; enlightening
Rigidity	stiff; inflexible; set in one's opinion or devoid of flexibility
Romantic	responsive to the idealized, heroic, adventurous or expressions of love or affection

S

Self-perpetuating	capable of indefinitely continuing or renewing itself
Stigma	discredited or shamed; specific diagnostic sign of a disease
Spiral	a continuously spreading and accelerating increase or decrease
Status quo	the existing state of affairs or conditions

T

Tarantula	a large, hairy American spider with a painful but not fatal bite
Terminal illness	fatal illness leading to death
Testify	give evidence, declare; acknowledge openly
Tongue-tied	unable or not inclined to speak freely; may be from shyness
Transition	change, movement, development or evolution from one form or stage to another

U

Under funded	provide insufficient funding for
Underlie	support; form the foundation or basis of

Underscore	stress, emphasize, make evident, underline
Unpredictable	uncertain or unable to indicate in advance on the basis of observation, experience or scientific reason

V

In a vacuum	a state of isolation from outside influences
Vehemently	intensely emotional, passionate; forcibly expressed

W

Ward	a large room in a hospital where patients requiring similar treatment are accommodated
Warehousing	confine or house a person in conditions suggestion of a room for storing merchandise
Wary	cautious; watchful, especially in detecting and escaping from danger
Wonder drug	miracle drug; relatively newly discovered drug that elicits a dramatic response in a patient's condition

Multiple Choice Posttest

After studying the text and completing the Study Guide activities, answer these questions to determine if you need to review any areas before the course exam.

1. Insight therapies focus on giving people _____.
   a. skills to change their behaviors
   b. clearer understanding of their feelings, motives, and actions
   c. an understanding of perceptual processes
   d. an understanding of biological influences on behavior

2. Neo-Freudians differ from traditional Freudian approaches to therapy in that they encourage clients to focus on the ____ and they favor ____ their clients.
   a. past; face-to-face discussions with
   b. present; face-to-face discussions with
   c. past; sitting behind and passively listening to
   d. present; sitting behind and passively listening to

3. The cardinal rule in client-centered therapy is for the therapist to express ____ for the client.
   a. unconditional positive regard
   b. conditional positive regard
   c. positive transference
   d. psychological congruence

4. Gestalt therapy emphasizes _____.
   a. the here-and-now
   b. face-to-face confrontations
   c. becoming more genuine in daily interactions
   d. All of the above

5. The main task of behavioral therapy is to _____.
   a. get the patient to look past the problem
   b. provide a warm atmosphere for discussing problems
   c. teach clients to behave in more effective ways
   d. provide insight into the causes of problems

6. The technique of _____ trains a client to remain relaxed and calm in the presence of a stimulus that he or she formerly feared.
   a. Reciprocal inhibition
   b. Free association
   c. Systematic desensitization
   d. Operant conditioning

7. Making someone who is afraid of snakes handle dozens of snakes in an effort to get him to overcome his fear is called _____.
   a. Systematic desensitization
   b. Flooding
   c. Paradoxical intent
   d. Aversive conditioning

8. In what type of therapy is a contract drawn up, binding both client and therapist as if they were involved in a legal agreement?
   a. Behavioral contracting
   b. Reciprocal inhibition
   c. Transactional analysis
   d. A token economy

9. Showing a client how his or her irrational and self-defeating beliefs are causing problems is MOST characteristic of ____ therapy.
   a. Psychoanalytic
   b. Behavioral
   c. Stress-inoculation
   d. Rational-emotive

10. Alcoholics Anonymous is an example of a (n)_____ group.
    a. encounter
    b. desensitization
    c. self-help
    d. structured behavior therapy

11. The psychotherapeutic approach that recognizes the value of a broad treatment package over a rigid commitment to one particular form of therapy is _____.
    a. Situationalism
    b. Existentialism
    c. Interactionism
    d. Eclecticism

12. In 1988, the new drug ___ was put on the market as the first of a new class of antidepressant drugs.
    a. Ecstasy
    b. Lithium
    c. Prozac
    d. Thorazine

13. Drugs that combat depression work by ____.
    a. Increasing the amount of serotonin in the brain
    b. Blocking dopamine receptors in the brain
    c. Inhibiting the function of the hypothalamus
    d. Increasing acetylcholine in the brain

14. Most antipsychotic drugs work by _____.
    a. Increasing acetylcholine in the brain
    b. Increasing the amount of serotonin in the brain
    c. Blocking dopamine receptors in the brain
    d. Inhibiting the function of the hypothalamus

15. Electroconvulsive therapy is most often used to alleviate ____.
    a. anxiety
    b. somatoform disorders
    c. schizophrenia
    d. severe depression

16. Which of the following treatments is LEAST likely to be used today?
    a. Electroconvulsive therapy
    b. Drug treatment
    c. Prefrontal lobotomy
    d. Behavioral therapy

17. Educating young people about AIDS through TV ad campaigns is a form of ___ prevention.
    a. basic
    b. primary
    c. tertiary
    d. secondary

18. Suicide hot lines and crisis intervention centers are all involved in ___ prevention.
    a. basic
    b. primary
    c. tertiary
    d. secondary

19. Halfway houses and other places where ex-patients can be supported in their efforts to return to normal life after release from institutions are forms of _____.
    a. basic
    b. primary
    c. tertiary
    d. secondary

Answers and Explanations to
Multiple Choice Posttest

1. b. Insight therapies are designed to give people better awareness and clearer understandings of their feelings, motivations and actions. p. 461

2. b. Many Neo-Freudian therapists encourage dealing with current situations and having face-to-face discussions. p. 463

3. a. The cardinal rule in client-centered therapy is for the therapist to express unconditional positive regard or true acceptance. p. 464

4. d. Gestalt therapy emphasizes the here and now, face-to-face confrontations and becoming more genuine in the client's daily life. p. 465

5. c. Behavior therapy's main task is to teach clients new and more satisfying ways of behaving. p. 467

6. c. Systematic desensitization gradually reduces fear and anxiety by association relaxation with the fearful stimuli. p. 467

7. b. Flooding involves full intensity exposure to a feared stimulus. p. 468

8. a. Behavioral contracting is a signed agreement between client and therapist regarding therapeutic goals and reinforcements. p. 469

9. d. Rational-emotive therapy (RET) is based on the idea that irrational and self-defeating beliefs cause psychological problems. p. 471

10. c. AA is the best-known self-help group. p. 473

11. d. Eclecticism recognizes the value of a broad treatment package over one form of therapy. p. 478

12. c. In 1988, Prozac was the first antidepressant drug to be introduced. p. 480

13. a. Antidepressant drugs, like Prozac, work by increasing the amount of serotonin in the brain. p. 480

14. c. Most antipsychotic drugs work by blocking dopamine receptors in the brain. p. 479

15. d. ECT is most often used for prolonged and severe depression when no other treatment is effective. p. 481

16. c. Prefrontal lobotomies are rarely performed today. p. 482

17. b. Programs that educate people about illness are forms of primary prevention. p. 485

18. d. Suicide hotlines and crisis intervention are forms of secondary prevention. p. 485

19. c. Halfway houses are a form of tertiary prevention. p. 485–6

Psychotherapy	Psychoanalysis
Insight therapy	Client-centered or person-centered therapy
Free association	Gestalt therapy
Transference	Short-term psycho-dynamic therapy
Insight	Behavior therapies

The theory of personality Freud developed as well as the form of therapy he invented.

The use of psychological techniques to treat personality and behavior disorders.

Nondirectional form of therapy developed by Carl Rogers that calls for unconditional positive regard of the client, by the therapist with the goal of helping the client become fully functioning.

A variety of individual psychotherapies designed to give people a better understanding of their feelings, motivations, and actions in the hope that this will help them adjust.

An insight therapy that emphasizes the wholeness of the personality and attempts to reawaken people to their emotions and sensations in the here-and-now.

A psychoanalytic technique that encourages the patient to talk without inhibition about whatever thoughts or fantasies come to mind.

Insight therapy that is time-limited and focused on trying to help clients correct the immediate problems in their lives.

The client's carrying over to the analyst feelings held toward childhood authority figure.

Therapeutic approaches that are based on the belief that all behavior, normal and abnormal, is learned, and that the objective of therapy is to teach people new, more satisfying ways of behaving.

Awareness of previously unconscious feelings and memories and how they influence present feelings and behavior.

Systematic desensitization	Cognitive therapies
Aversive conditioning	Stress-inoculation therapy
Behavior contracting	Rational-emotive therapy (RET)
Token economy	Cognitive therapy
Modeling	Group therapy

Psychotherapies that emphasize changing clients' perceptions of their life situations as a way of modifying their behavior.

A behavioral technique for reducing a person's fear and anxiety by gradually associating a new response (relaxation) with stimuli that have been causing the fear and anxiety.

A type of cognitive therapy that trains clients to cope with stressful situations by learning a more useful pattern of self-talk.

Behavior therapy techniques aimed at eliminating undesirable behavior patterns by teaching the person to associate them with pain and discomfort.

A directive cognitive therapy based on the idea that clients' psychological distress is caused by irrational and self-defeating beliefs and that the therapist's job is to challenge such dysfunctional beliefs.

Form of operant conditioning therapy in which the client and therapist set behavioral goals and agree on reinforcements the client will receive on reaching those goals.

Therapy that depends on identifying and changing inappropriately negative and self-critical patterns of thought.

An operant conditioning therapy in which patients earn tokens (reinforcers) for desired behaviors and exchange them for desired items or privileges.

Type of psychotherapy in which clients meet regularly to interact and help one another achieve insight into their feelings and behavior.

A behavior therapy in which the person learns desired behaviors by watching others perform those behaviors.

Family therapy	Electroconvulsive therapy (ECT)
Couple therapy	Psychosurgery
Eclecticism	Deinstitutionalization
Biological treatments	Primary prevention
Antipsychotic drugs	Secondary prevention

Biological therapy in which a mild electrical current is passed through the brain for a short period, often producing convulsions and temporary coma; used to treat severe, prolonged depression.

A form of group therapy that sees the family as at least partly responsible for the individual's problems and seeks to change all family members' behaviors to the benefit of the family unit as well as the troubled invididual.

Brain surgery performed to change a person's behavior or emotional state; a biological therapy rarely used today.

Form of group therapy intended to help troubled partners improve their problems of communication and interaction.

Policy of treating people with severe psychological disorders in the larger community, or in small residential centers such as halfway houses, rather than in large public hospitals.

Psychotherapeutic approach that recognizes the value of a broad treatment package over a rigid commitment to one particular form of therapy.

Techniques and programs to improve the social environment so that new cases of mental disorders do not develop.

Group of approaches, including medication, electroconvulsive therapy, and psychosurgery, that are sometimes used to treat psychological disorders in conjunction with, or instead of, psychotherapy.

Programs to identify groups that are at high risk for mental disorders and to detect maladaptive behavior in these groups and treat it promptly.

Drugs used to treat very severe psychological disorders, particularly schizophrenia.

Tertiary
prevention

Programs to help people
adjust to community life
after release from a mental
hospital.

14 Social Psychology

Use this section for class and text notes. Distinguish between lecture notes, textbook concepts, topics emphasized on the exams and your own comments.

1.   Social Cognition   page 495

   A. Forming Impressions

   - Schemata

      – Schema

      – Self-fulfilling prophecy

   - Stereotypes

   B. Attribution

   - Explaining Behavior

      – Attribution Theory

   - Biases

      – Fundamental attribution error

      – Defensive attribution

      – Just-world hypotheses

   - Attribution across Cultures

C. Interpersonal Attraction

- Proximity

- Physical attractiveness

- Similarity

- Exchange

- Intimacy

---

2.   Attitudes p. 503

A. The Nature of Attitudes

- Attitudes and behaviors

  - Self-monitoring

  - Attitude development

B. Prejudice and Discrimination

- Prejudice

- Discrimination

- Sources of Prejudice

  - Frustration-aggression theory

  - Authoritarian personality

  - Racism

  - Reducing prejudice

- Recategorize

- Controlled processing

- Conditions

C. Changing Attitudes

- The process of persuasion

- The communication model

- Cognitive dissonance theory

UNDERSTANDING the World Around Us   page 508–9

Ethnic Conflict and Violence

- Propaganda

- Shared collective memories

- Personal and social identity

- Societal beliefs

---

3.   Social Influence   page 514

A. Cultural Influences

- Norm

B. Conformity

- Size of group

- Unanimity

- Nature of the task

- Conformity across Cultures

Learning Objectives and Questions

After you have read and studied this chapter, you should be able to complete the following statements. Your exam is written based on these learning objectives.

OBJECTIVES:

1. Describe the process by which we form first impressions of other people. Identify three factors that influence personal perception.

2. Explain three aspects of attribution and explain attribution errors.

3. Explain the dynamics of interpersonal attraction.

4. Identify the components of attitudes. Explain how attitudes are acquired and how they change.

5. Explain the origin of prejudice and discrimination and how prejudice can be reduced.

6. Discuss the dynamics of attitude change and the process of persuasion.

7. Explain the theory of cognitive dissonance.

8. Explain how culture, conformity, compliance, and obedience exert social influence.

9. Identify the four types of social action.

10. Define risky shift and polarization. Summarize the conditions under which groups are effective and ineffective in solving problems.

11. Identify at least two theories of leadership.

12. Identify the focus and goals of industrial/organizational psychology.

Language Support

Students identified the following words from the text as needing more explanation. This page can be cut-out, folded in half, and used as a bookmark for this chapter.

A

Acquiesce — to go along with, comply or submit, usually after thoughtful consideration

Astray — away from what is desired; in error

Ambiguity — having more than one interpretation or meanings

Ally — one that's associated with another as a helper

B

Bigoted — stubbornly and intolerantly devoted to one's own opinions and prejudices

Blatantly — obvious, in a noisy, offensive, crude manner

Bribe — something that influences or causes behavior to occur

C

Chance encounter — to come upon unexpectedly

Candor — free from prejudice or malice; fair, impartial, honest

Chalk up — to attribute or credit as a cause

Concerted effort — mutually agreed upon, planned or devised

Credibility — quality or power of inspiring belief

Conspire — plot; act in harmony toward a common end

D

Deep-rooted — firmly implanted or established

Decipher — to interpret or figure out meaning although indistinct

Door-to-door — going to each house in a neighborhood

Dissenter — one who differs in opinion

E

Ethos — distinguishing character, sentiment, moral nature or guiding beliefs of a person, group or institution

Entice — tempt; to attract by arousing hope or desire

Eloquent — marked by forceful and fluent expression; articulate communicator

Endorsement — to approve of by expressing support or approval, often publicly

F

Flesh out — make fuller or more nearly complete

Fuss over — show of flattering attention

Flattery — insincere or excessive praise

G

Gamut — whole series or entire range or scope

Genocide — the deliberate and systematic destruction of a racial, political or cultural group

Gist — essence, main point or part

Gossip — rumor or report about others; usually personal or sensational

H

Holocaust — mass slaughter of Europeans, especially Jews, by the Nazis in WWII

Hardheaded — stubborn, willful; realistic; concerned with practical considerations

Harbor — hold persistently in the mind; provide refuge for

I

Illegitimate	not recognized as lawful offspring; born of parents who aren't married to each other
Inculcate	teach and impress by repetition, counsel, advice or caution
Idolize	love or admire to excess; to worship
Indecisive	uncertain how to act or proceed; indefinite

L

Lenient	mind and tolerant disposition

M

Mumble	utter words in a low, confused, indistinct manner
Malign	to give misleading or false reports about
Mandated	by formal order; directed or required by the court
Malevolent	having or showing intense, often vicious, ill will, spite or hatred
Mar	detract from the perfection or wholeness of

N

In a nutshell	in a very brief statement
Naïve	lacking wisdom or informed judgment; with unaffected simplicity

O

Oppress	exercise harsh authority or power over; subdue, restrain; weigh heavily on the mind
Ostensibly	to all outward appearances; apparently; open to view

P

Paramount	prevailing over others; dominant; having superior position
Pegged	identified
Polite	showing correct social usage; considerate; tactful; courteous
Plight	unfortunate, difficult, uncertain or dangerous situation
Put-downs	humiliating remark; degrade or belittle

R

Rally	mass meeting intended to arouse group enthusiasm
Rhetoric	art of speaking or writing effectively; skillful communication

S

Stethoscope	instrument used to detect and study sounds produced in the body
Speculation	ponder on a subject; review something casually and often without conclusions
Scare tactics	gaining an advantage by spreading alarm or fear
Solidarity	unity; based on common interests, objectives and standards
Old standby	something which one can rely on; a favorite and available choice
Steeped in	subject thoroughly in some strong or dominating influence
Single file	a row of people or things arranged one behind the other
Stranger	unknown person who one is not acquainted with
Scenarios	hypothetical or imagined sequence of events; account or summary of possible courses of actions or events

T

Truism	undoubted or self-evident truth; one too obvious to mention

U

Unforeseen	not seen or known in advance; not predicted or discerned

V

Violate	to do harm to, especially sexually; fail to show respect for
Vested	special concern or stake in maintaining or influencing something for selfish ends
Vent	to give vigorous or emotional expression to

W

Wanton	hard to control, playfully mean or cruel; inhumane

Multiple Choice Posttest

After studying the text and completing the Study Guide activities, answer these questions to determine if you need to review any areas before the course exam.

1. The process by which others individually or collectively affect one's perceptions, attitudes and action.
   a. Group dynamics
   b. Social influence
   c. Conformity
   d. Culture

2. Whenever a person has two contradictory cognitions at the same time, a state of _____ exists.
   a. cognitive congruence
   b. nonreciprocity
   c. cognitive dissonance
   d. creative conflict

3. The person who conducted the most well-known research on obedience is _____.
   a. Asch
   b. Milgram
   c. Luchens
   d. Kelley

4. _____ behavior is helping other people with no expectation of personal gain.
   a. Reciprocal
   b. Deindividuated
   c. Diffused
   d. Altruistic

5. The _____ effect is that people are more likely to comply with a second, larger request after complying with a first, small request.
   a. response cue
   b. bait and switch
   c. foot-in-the-door
   d. primacy

6. _____ is a process by which people feel anonymous in a large group.
   a. deindividuation
   b. identity moratorium
   c. identity diffusion
   d. groupthink

7. The tendency for an individual's helpfulness in an emergency to decrease as the number of bystanders increases is called _____.
   a. the risky shift phenomenon
   b. groupthink
   c. the bystander effect
   d. social loafing

8. In a mob, one dominant person can often convince people to act due to the _____ effect.
   a. lowball
   b. snowball
   c. primacy
   d. door-in-the-face

9. The poor decisions made in the Watergate cover-up, the Challenger disaster and the Bay of Pigs invasion were due primarily to _____.
   a. groupthink
   b. deindividuation
   c. risky shift
   d. polarization

10. The focus of industrial/organizational psychology is _____.
    a. Strategies for founding an economically successful business
    b. Behavior in organizational settings
    c. The effects of industrialization on the environment
    d. Personal problems of employed persons

11. Most of us associate _____ with good personality traits, intelligence, and happiness.
    a. youth
    b. attractiveness
    c. old age
    d. wealth

12. The most important factor in interpersonal attraction is _____.
    a. proximity
    b. similarity
    c. attractiveness
    d. reciprocity

13. Rebecca consistently expresses her beliefs with a little regard for the constraints imposed by the situation. She is probably a _____ self-monitor.
    a. reactive
    b. nonreactive
    c. low
    d. high

14. According to attribution theory, people ___ for good situations and ____ for bad ones.
    a. take credit; take credit
    b. deny responsibility; deny responsibility
    c. take credit; deny responsibility
    d. deny responsibility; take credit

15. Bad things happen to bad people and good things happen to good people, according to _____.
    a. the self-serving bias
    b. the just-world hypothesis
    c. the self-fulfilling prophecy
    d. the reciprocity model

16. Each of the following is a promising strategy for reducing prejudice and discrimination EXCEPT _____.
    a. Recategorization
    b. Controlled processing
    c. Improving contact between groups
    d. Increased competition between groups

17. The number one health hazard for college students is _____.
    a. binge drinking
    b. AIDS and other STDs
    c. smoking
    d. illegal drug use

18. People who risked their lives to save persecuted Jews from the Holocaust shared one specific characteristic: _____.
    a. They saw their behavior as normal, not heroic
    b. They all came from powerful, wealthy families
    c. They were all highly educated
    d. They tended to come from working-class families.

Answers and Explanations to Multiple Choice Posttest

1. b. Social Influence is the process by which others individually or collectively affect one's perceptions, attitudes and actions. p. 514

2. c. Cognitive dissonance occurs when a person has two contradictory cognitions at the same time. p. 512–3

3. d. Milgram has conducted the most well-known research on obedience. p. 519

4. d. Altruistic behavior seeks no personal gain. p. 521

5. c. The foot-in-the-door effect occurs when people comply with a second larger request after complying first with a small request. p. 518

6. a. Deindividuation is the process by which people feel anonymous in a large group. p. 521

7. c. The bystander effect occurs when an increase in the number of bystanders decreases the likelihood than an individual in the group will be helpful. p. 521

8. b. The snowball effect occurs when a dominant person in a mob is able to convince people to act. p. 521

9. a. Groupthink occurs when there is so much pressure from the group to conform that people don't feel free to express critical ideas. p. 525

10. b. The focus of industrial/organizational psychology is behavior in organized settings. p. 526

11. b. Most people associate attractiveness with good personality traits, intelligence, and happiness. p. 500

12. a. Proximity or how close people live to each other, is the most important factor in interpersonal attraction. p. 500

13. c. Rebecca is a low self-monitor. p. 505

14. c. People take credit for good situations and deny responsibility for bad ones, according to attribution theory. p. 498

15. b. The just world hypothesis holds that bad things happen to bad people and good things happen to good people. p. 499

16. d. Increased competition between groups is not a promising strategy for reducing prejudice and discrimination. p. 507–10

17. a. Binge drinking is the number one health hazard for college students. p. 517

18. a. People who risked their lives to save persecuted Jews during the Holocaust all saw their behavior as normal and not heroic. p. 523

Key Vocabulary Terms

Cut out each term and use as study cards.
Definition is on the back side of each term.

Social psychology	Fundamental attribution error
Primacy effect	Defensive attribution
Self-fulfilling prophecy	Just-world hypothesis
Stereotype	Proximity
Attribution theory	Exchange

Tendency of people to overemphasize personal causes for other people's behavior and to underemphasize personal causes for their own behavior.	Scientific study of the ways in which the thoughts, feelings, and behaviors of one individual are influenced by the real, imagined, or inferred behavior or characteristics of other people.
Tendency to attribute our successes to our own efforts or qualities and our failures to external factors.	The fact that early information about someone weighs more heavily than later information in influencing one's impression of that person.
Attribution error based on the assumption that bad things happen to bad people and good things happen to good people.	Process in which a person's expectation about another elicits behavior from the second person that confirms the expectation.
How close two people live to each other.	Set of characteristics presumed to be shared by all members of a social category.
Concept that relationships are based on trading rewards among partners.	Theory that addresses the question of how people make judgments about the causes of behavior.

Equity	Frustration-aggression theory
Attitude	Authoritarian personality
Self-monitoring	Racism
Prejudice	Cognitive dissonance
Discrimination	Social influence

Theory that under certain circumstances people who are frustrated in their goals turn their anger away from the proper powerful target and toward a less powerful target because it is safer to attack.

Fairness of exchange achieved when each partner in the relationship receives the same proportion of outcomes to investments.

A personality pattern characterized by rigid conventionality, exaggerated respect for authority, and hostility toward those who defy society's norms.

Relatively stable organization of beliefs, feelings, and behavior tendencies directed toward something or someone-the attitude object.

Prejudice and discrimination directed at a particular racial group.

Tendency for an individual to observe the situation for cues about how to react.

Perceived inconsistency between two cognitions.

An unfair, intolerant, or unfavorable attitude toward a group of people.

Process by which others individually or collectively affect one's perceptions, attitudes, and actions.

An unfair act or series of acts taken toward an entire group of people or individual members of that group.

Norm	Altruistic behavior
Conformity	Bystander effect
Compliance	Risky shift
Obedience	Polarization
Deindividuation	Great person theory

Helping behavior that is not linked to personal gain.	A shared idea or expectation about how to behave.
Greater willingness of a group than an individual to take substantial risks.	Voluntarily yielding to social norms, even at the expense of one's preferences.
Greater willingness to take risks in decision making in a group than as independent individuals.	Change of behavior in response to an explicit request from another person or group.
Shift in attitudes by members of a group toward more extreme positions than the ones held before group discussion.	Change of behavior in response to a command from another person, typically an authority figure.
Theory that leadership is a result of personal qualities and traits that qualify one to lead others.	Loss of personal sense of responsibility in a group.

Industrial/ organization psychology	
Hawthorne effect	
Social cognition	
Schema	

	Area of psychology concerned with the application of psychological principles to the problems of human organizations, especially work organizations.
	Principle that subjects will alter their behavior because of researcher's attention and not necessarily because of any specific treatment condition.
	Knowledge and understanding concerning the social world and the people in it (including oneself).
	A set of beliefs or expectations about something that is based on past experiences.